Finding Common Ground:
Service-Learning and Education Reform

A Survey of 28 Leading School Reform Models

Sarah S. Pearson

The University of New Mexico
At Gallup

Table of Contents

FOREWORD

As is the case in all our work, the American Youth Policy Forum seeks to bridge the fields of youth policy, practice and research in order to establish a base of common knowledge among experts in these respective areas. We attempt to improve opportunities and outcomes for young people by cutting across silos of information and special interest, which tend to dictate how programs and interventions for young people are perceived, implemented and supported. With this report, *Finding Common Ground: Service-Learning and Education Reform*, which looks at comprehensive school reform models through the lens of service-learning, we hope to provide a new perspective on the use of and implications for this rich learning methodology that integrates community service with academic study to enhance learning, teach civic responsibility and strengthen communities.

As policymakers and practitioners grapple with the demanding, technical, and sometimes creative work of school reform, we hope that they will find in this publication useful ways of thinking about service-learning and useful applications for fulfilling their charge. We know of the enduring benefits of service-learning, both motivational and academic, as well as its utility as a mechanism for providing alternative ways of learning.

The report provides insights from researchers, practitioners, and comprehensive school reform developers and implementers on how these models work and their underlying assumptions. It also provides their frank assessments about how compatible the models are with the basic principles of service-learning. Where a model is not specifically using service-learning strategies, recommendations are provided for how these strategies can easily support or be infused within the model's existing design.

Though the language and the terms used in many of the models may differ from those typically used in service-learning, it soon becomes clear that many of the underlying principles are the same. There is much to be learned from each camp; there is even more to be derived from combining the cumulative knowledge that both bring in support of better schooling opportunities and improved outcomes—academic, social, civic and economic—for all our young people.

Glenda Partee and Betsy Brand, Co-directors
American Youth Policy Forum

INTRODUCTION

Educating the Whole Student – Heart and Head

This guide for policymakers at the national, state, local, and school levels illuminates common ground between two dynamic movements—education reform and service-learning—often viewed as existing in separate worlds. Comprehensive school reform models are working to systematically improve the education of children and youth based on scientifically based research and effective practices. Quality service-learning, executed by thoughtful teachers and monitored by diligent principals, completes the fundamental mission of education by stimulating children and youth to act as responsible and participating members of the community. Service-learning links community service to academics, building an ethos or characteristic spirit and belief of service to others. Effective comprehensive school reform models in many communities are already integrating service-learning or elements of service-learning.

Finding Common Ground: Service-Learning and Education Reform encourages the inclusion of service-learning as a viable partner in education reform and revitalization efforts. It advises further research as to how service-learning can support the academic school reform movement to educate students in a truly comprehensive way—heart as well as head. The reader will find an analysis of leading school reform models with a focus on their compatibility with service-learning. Also included is a description of how models ranked themselves against essential service-learning elements, a brief description of both service-learning and comprehensive school reform, suggestions on how these two initiatives could work more closely together, and examples of barriers that must first be overcome.

Leading school reform models were selected from among the comprehensive school reform models listed in the original Comprehensive School Reform Demonstration (CSRD) program established by Congress in 1998. A self-scoring, 12-question survey with space provided for comments on key service-learning elements was sent to model developers and up to four schools per model that had used the model for at least two years. A majority of the 28 models surveyed rated as "compatible" with service-learning; 11 rated as "highly compatible;" three rated as "somewhat compatible;" and one rated as "neutral." A summary analysis of each model was developed from current information and research, comments provided by model developers, and comments provided by schools using the model. A chart of compatibility for all school reform models, broken down by key service-learning element, can be found in the Appendix. Not surprisingly, some models scored themselves high on some questions, but offered little to substantiate their claim. The truth comes out in the summary analysis.

The quest to unite these two worlds is not new. Education reformers and service-learning leaders teamed up in 1995 at a joint meeting between the U.S. Department of Education and the Corporation for National Service (now the Corporation for National and Community Service). This group representing more than 30 states, came together to discuss steps to bring about school improvement by developing closer linkages between schools and their communities. A *Declaration of Principles* emerged from the meeting. (An abridged version of the Principles and an action agenda for each is listed in the Appendix.) This American Youth Policy Forum (AYPF) publication revisits the concepts underlying those Principles and shows how some leading school reform models are turning Principles into effective practice, integrating school improvement and service-learning.

There is a greater need now, more than ever, for education reformers to welcome service-learning as a respected partner in education. Service-learning is gaining recognition among educators, policymakers, foundations, and students as a way to connect back to and be a part of the community.

The compatibility highlighted in the following summaries of school reform models can and should be leveraged by schools to educate and prepare youth to be effective workers, family members, and informed and engaged citizens. Findings in this study pinpoint distinct areas for further collaboration between service-learning and school reform efforts and highlight opportunities for building a stronger, more comprehensive education program for the whole child.

WHAT IS SERVICE-LEARNING?

The National Commission on Service-Learning, chaired by former United States Senator John Glenn, and sponsored by the W. K. Kellogg Foundation to study the practice of service-learning in America's schools describes service-learning as *"an innovative teaching methodology that integrates community service with academic study to enrich learning, teach civic responsibility and strengthen communities."* According to a recent report by the Commission, research shows that when students are involved in quality service-learning they make gains on achievement tests and increase their grade point averages. The Commission writes that service-learning accomplishes the following:

- Reverses **student disengagement** from schooling by giving students responsibility for their own learning and increasing their motivation to participate in school activities.
- Reinforces and extends the **standards-based reform** movement by providing a real-life context for learning and giving students a sense of the practical importance of what they are learning in school.
- Promotes the **public purposes of education** by preparing students for citizenship through involvement in citizen action.
- Builds on the growing **willingness of students to become involved in service** to their communities while adding an academic component to such service.
- Contributes to young people's **personal and career development** by reducing violence and sexual activity and increasing their sense of responsibility and workplace skills (2002, p. 4).

The term "service-learning" was defined in federal legislation for the first time in the National and Community Service Act of 1990. The Act's definition of service-learning is specific and allows schools, as well as community-based organizations, to provide service-learning activities or projects for students:

> The term 'service-learning' means a method under which students or participants learn and develop through active participation in thoughtfully organized service that:
> - is conducted in and meets the needs of a community; is coordinated with an elementary school, secondary school, institution of higher education, or community service program, and with the community; and helps foster civic responsibility; and
> - is integrated into and enhances the academic curriculum of the students, or the educational components of the community service program in which the participants are enrolled; and provides structured time for the students or participants to reflect on the service experience" (Section 101 (23)).

Service-learning can be used to increase and retain academic skills in mathematics, writing, reading, social studies, science, language, and other studies. It may not be appropriate for each and every educational experience, for example when students are learning the basics of sentence structure, or the rules of multiplication or division. However, with foresight and careful planning, service-learning can create an overarching theme for the curriculum that engages students in purposeful learning and gives them an opportunity to apply what they are learning to a challenging situation or problem in their community. Service-learning expands the learning environment beyond the limitations of a classroom, making an impression on students that lives on after the quizzes and tests are over. It provides the essential connection that helps students see that *what* they are learning in class *is* relevant to the world around them.

Service-learning, says Professor Janet Mason of the College of Education, University of South Carolina, is one of the best tools for engaging the "reluctant learner," a student who is disengaged from the learning process. Mason, a former teacher and middle school vice principal, believes that teachers must be prepared to engage all learners. She requires her undergraduate students to complete service-learning activities in community agencies and alternative learning settings. There, her student teachers are empowered to develop and explore their own humanity, learn what it means to be multi-cultural, develop self-esteem, and face up to their own values. Through service-learning, Mason's students master a powerful methodology for engaging all learners, overcome any reluctance or fear they might have about the relationship between teaching and community engagement, and learn to appreciate the importance of service-learning to their effectiveness as a professional. As part of certification, the prestigious National Board for Professional Teaching Standards requires evidence of how teachers connect to community and parents.

Service-learning activities can be integrated into the curriculum and aligned with state and local content and performance standards (sometimes known as frameworks). Units of study or lesson plans that are driven by service-learning and linked to standards can introduce compelling issues that grasp student interest. Units on neighborhood and community health, homelessness, and natural disasters, for example, are being taught in Wisconsin schools. Boston Public Schools is "connecting classrooms, communities and careers," linking their school-to-careers program with service-learning to create standards-driven units or lesson plans such as: Make Smoking History, Honor Veterans, and Learn to Teach–Teach to Learn. An Oregon community-based organization called Stop Oregon Litter and Vandalism (SOLV) promotes units of study such as School Litter, Litter at Home, Garbage Melt-Down, and The Cost of Vandalism. The Vermont Framework of Standards and Learning Opportunities provides a curriculum planning and assessment tool for teachers to help them align standards with learning opportunities and assessment strategies. These examples along with a curriculum-building tool can be accessed in the Education Commission of the States' *Service-Learning and Standards Toolkit—Achieving Academic Excellence Through Serving Communities*. The Toolkit is a teaching and learning strategy that enhances standards-based education, allowing students to apply curriculum content to real issues or problems in their community. It guides educators on using service-learning to provide opportunities for students to see the interconnectedness of curriculum areas and the ways in which content standards weave together.

Academics, Civic Engagement, Character Building: A Comprehensive Approach

Developing a lesson plan or unit of study that guides students to apply academic skills to real world problems takes thoughtful planning and yields powerful and long-lasting student learning. It is a strategy that builds character, spurs civic engagement, and applies context to abstract theories, allowing teachers to engage students as active participants in the learning process. Instead of simply asking students to open their textbooks, teachers using service-learning engage students in a critical thinking exercise to examine their world. Students are guided to connect their interests and moral leadership to solve a problem, serve a need, or be of service to others. Once a focus for service is identified, students may apply skills such as data collection, documentation, problem-solving, charting and graphing, and persuasive writing to test theories, develop surveys, analyze data, inform community decision-makers, and practice presentation skills. Service-learning can be woven into the curriculum through a variety of instructional methods: problem-based, project-based, place-based, work-based, school-based enterprise, mentoring, applied learning, contextual learning, or character education. Most school models described in this guide use at least one or a combination of these methods.

Service-Learning Nationwide: A Sleeping Giant

Service-learning is growing quietly—as some would say, a "sleeping giant" (Bhaerman, Cordell & Gomez, 1998, p. 70) alongside the nation's burgeoning education reform movement. In 1999, a study by the National Center for Educational Statistics, *Service-Learning and Community Service in K-12 Public Schools*, asked schools to report on the use of service-learning in the curriculum as well as on their engagement in community service. The study revealed that 32 percent of all public schools organize service-learning as part of their curriculum, including almost half of all high schools. "Most schools with service-learning cited strengthening relationships among students, the school, and the community as key reasons for practicing service-learning" (Skinner, R. & Chapman C., 1999, p. 1).

Federal and private foundation investment has helped to spread service-learning nationwide. Private foundations such as the W. K. Kellogg Foundation, DeWitt Wallace Readers' Digest Fund, and the Carnegie Corporation provided some of the initial funding to national nonprofit organizations to expand quality service-learning. *Learning in Deed*, a service-learning initiative supported by the W. K. Kellogg Foundation, awarded grants to states to assess the effectiveness of service-learning in schools and community-based organizations and to strengthen related policies at the state, district, and local levels. *Learn and Serve America*, a federal grant program within the Corporation for National and Community Service, funds service-learning initiatives in schools and community organizations across the country. *National Service-Learning Leader Schools*, a program of Learn and Serve America, showcases schools in nearly every state that demonstrate a high level of quality service-learning integrated throughout the school's curriculum.

National associations are tuning into service-learning, noting the added value it offers their constituents. The Association for Supervision and Curriculum Development (ASCD) has recognized service-learning as a "widespread and permanent fixture of the educational landscape" (Gene Carter, ASCD press release January 31, 2002). The Education Commission of the States (ECS) and the Compact for Learning and Citizenship (CLC) have recognized its influence on important education policy goals, such as increasing student retention and motivation, creating a safe learning environment, helping young people become competent citizens, and improving school and community relations, as shared in their *Service-Learning and Standards Toolkit—Achieving Academic Excellence Through Serving Communities* (2001).

Service-learning programs exist in every state while California and Maryland have established service-learning goals for <u>all</u> students (Billig, S. H., May 2000). Oregon, South Carolina, Massachusetts, California, Minnesota, and Maine have received federal and foundation grants to support the integration of service-learning into their public school curriculum and are leading the way with supportive policies that serve as service-learning beacons. Cities such as Atlanta, Chicago, Philadelphia, and Washington strongly encourage or mandate service-learning for their students. States such as South Carolina, Delaware, Kentucky, and Vermont strongly promote service-learning as a strategy for education reform. Examples of quality service-learning and supportive state and local policies have been captured in forum briefs and field trip reports on the American Youth Policy Forum's web site, www.aypf.org.

Out of this growth in the field, a national leadership organization, the National Service-Learning Partnership (NSLP) has formed. The Partnership is dedicated to advancing service-learning as a core element of the educational experience for every elementary, middle, and secondary school student in the United States. In an effort to help schools integrate service fully into curriculum, NSLP provides critical leadership for communications effectiveness, legislative advocacy, knowledge exchange, organizational collaboration, marketing savvy, and practice excellence. The Partnership brings together organizations and individuals, including thousands of practitioners, administrators, community leaders, policymakers, researchers, parents, and young people.

WHAT IS COMPREHENSIVE SCHOOL REFORM?

Comprehensive School Reform (CSR), formerly Comprehensive School Reform Demonstration Programs—CSRD, is a federal program incorporated under the reauthorization of the Elementary and Secondary Education Act, the No Child Left Behind Act of 2002. CSR legislation provides financial incentives for schools to develop and implement comprehensive reform programs. Schools compete for these federal funds to adopt or develop research-based comprehensive reform approaches that employ innovative strategies and proven methods. Schools that adopt a CSR program, also known as "model" or "design," must show that they can implement schoolwide reform plans that follow the features listed. CSR programs build upon what the field knows about how children learn and combine this knowledge with best instructional practices. CSR programs provide a cohesive and comprehensive plan for education reform, not a fragmented approach that, in the past, has failed to raise or sustain higher student achievement. To be considered a CSR program, a school model should adequately address the following eleven components [as seen in the legislation]:

1. Employs proven strategies based on scientifically based research and effective practices.
2. Integrates a comprehensive design for effective school functioning, including instruction, assessment, classroom management, professional development, parental involvement, and school management, that aligns the school's curriculum, technology, and professional development into a comprehensive school reform plan, and state content and student academic achievement standards.
3. Provides high quality teacher and staff professional development.
4. Includes measurable goals for academic achievement and benchmarks for meeting the goals.
5. Is supported by the school's staff.
6. Provides support for staff.
7. **Provides for meaningful involvement of parents and the local community in planning, implementing, and evaluating school improvement activities.** [Emphasis added]
8. Uses high quality external technical support and assistance.
9. Plans for an annual evaluation of implementation.
10. Identifies other resources to sustain reform efforts.
11. Has been found, through scientifically based research, to significantly improve the academic achievement of students.

Component 7, community involvement, has been highlighted to bring attention to the fact that truly comprehensive school reform models must include the community in their school reform design. The degree of involvement, however, is not defined in the original CSRD or in the updated version of CSR as incorporated into the No Child Left Behind Act of 2002.

According to education reformer Margaret Wang and other writers of *What Do We Know*, a report analyzing 12 widely implemented school improvement programs, "…reform programs are of two types: comprehensive or curricular. Comprehensive school reform programs focus on school governance and organization and may also include emphasis on revised curricular content. Curricular reform programs emphasize content in one or more academic disciplines" (Wang, M. C., Haertel, G. D., & Walberg, H. J., 1997, p. 1). Some school models connect learning to the physical and psychological development of the child, as seen in Wang's school model design, Community for Learning and James Comer's School Development Program. Some school models, such as Coalition of Essential Schools and Accelerated Schools assess student learning in new ways, including portfolios and exhibitions. Some models, such as Integrated Thematic Instruction and The Learning Network, focus mainly on the teacher as the source for reform. Still, other models dive deeply into areas of philosophy and process in school governance, curriculum instruction, and professional development, such as America's Choice and High Schools That Work.

SURVEY FINDINGS

The 28 leading school reform models that participated in the study represent the general field of school reform. Through their survey responses and compatibility ratings with 12 key service-learning elements (listed on p. 15), they provide the shared information that can help align the two worlds of service-learning and education reform. The large number of leading school models scoring as "highly compatible" with key service-learning elements demonstrates an atmosphere of great support for service-learning, reinforcing the idea that significant common ground exists between service-learning advocates and education reformers.

Leading school model developers view the following service-learning elements as *highly compatible*:

1) Teachers use a variety of learning materials other than textbooks.

2) Opportunities are provided for students to apply their knowledge and skills to real-life situations and problems.

3) Alternative assessments such as portfolios, presentations and rubrics are used.

4) Time is provided for student reflection in journal entries and classroom dialog.

The following service-learning elements are viewed as *compatible*:

1) Instructional methods that include project-based learning.

2) Flexible use of time such as block scheduling.

3) Alternative teaching strategies such as project-based learning and applied learning.

4) Interdisciplinary team teaching and/or experiential learning methods.

5) Curriculum that addresses specific local community needs.

6) Students play a role in planning curricular activities. It should be noted that the last element listed scored low in "compatibility," nearly falling into the "somewhat compatible" zone.

One service-learning element, curriculum objectives for developing civic skills and competencies, is viewed as *somewhat compatible*.

Finally, one question that asks whether the model addresses school and district policy on students' ability to leave school grounds to attend outside learning activities was left unanswered by many school model developers, and scored low by others. This represents the only major hurdle to the integration of service-learning and school reform identified in the survey. School or district policy that inhibits the ability of students to leave school grounds will undermine the success of many service-learning projects. However, almost half of the models in the study have already successfully addressed this policy issue with schools and districts and scored it as *compatible* or *highly compatible*, including: Accelerated Schools, Audrey Cohen College, Coalition of Essential Schools, Expeditionary/Outward Bound, High Schools That Work, Integrated Thematic Instruction, League of Professional Schools, MicroSociety, Paideia, QuESt, School Development Program, Talent Development, and Ventures Education Systems.

Eleven school models scored as *highly compatible* overall. Some models have the same combined score for all 12 questions. For example, Coalition of Essential Schools and League of Professional Schools ranked at the top with the highest scores. They were followed closely by Integrated Thematic Instruction and Expeditionary Outward Bound. Models that scored as *somewhat compatible* did find some service-learning elements that were "compatible" or "highly compatible" with their school design. Some models scored themselves low on questions that asked about curriculum because their model does not prescribe a curriculum. As mentioned earlier, some model developers scored themselves high on some questions, and their claims were vetted in the summary analysis of their design.

SUMMARIES

The following pages provide summary of 28 leading school models responding to the study's 12-question survey (see Appendix). The models in the study were selected from those listed in the original Comprehensive School Reform Demonstration Program Act of 1998.

- Accelerated Schools Project
- America's Choice School Design
- ATLAS Communities
- Audrey Cohen College
- Center for Effective Schools
- Coalition of Essential Schools
- Community for Learning
- Community Learning Centers
- Co-Nect Schools
- Core Knowledge
- Different Ways of Knowing
- Direct Instruction
- Expeditionary Learning/Outward Bound
- Foxfire Fund
- High Schools That Work
- HighScope Primary Grades Approach to Education
- Integrated Thematic Instruction
- League of Professional Schools
- Learning Network
- MicroSociety
- Modern Red School House
- Onward to Excellence II
- Paideia
- Quest
- Roots and Wings (Success for All)
- School Development Program
- Talent Development
- Ventures Education Systems Corporation

Scoring Process

Scores were totaled for all 12 questions. The totaled score translated to a rating of compatibility. A breakdown of how each model scored per question can be found in the Appendix.

SCORE	RESPONSE	COMPATIBILITY
4.5-5	strong yes	Highly Compatible
3.5-4.4	yes	Compatible
2.5-3.4	on the way	Somewhat Compatible
1.5-2.4	don't know, or not applicable	Neutral
0	no	Not Compatible

School Reform Model Rankings
Compatibility with Service-Learning

Highly Compatible (4.5 – 5)

Coalition of Essential Schools	5
League of Professional Schools	5
Integrated Thematic Instruction	4.91
Expeditionary Learning Outward	4.83
Accelerated	4.75
Different Ways of Knowing	4.75
Microsociety	4.75
Audrey Cohen College	4.58
Paideia	4.58
Center for Effective Schools	4.5
Co-nect	4.5

Compatible (3.5 – 4.4)

High/Scope	4.33
School Development Program	4.33
Atlas Communities	4.16
Community for Learning	4.16
High Schools That Work	4
Modern Red Schoolhouse	4
Community Learning Centers	3.91
Core Knowledge	3.91
Ventures	3.75
America's Choice	3.66
Learning Network	3.66
QuESt	3.66
Direct Instruction	3.5

Somewhat Compatible (2.5 – 3.4)

Roots and Wings	3.41
Talent Development	3.41
Foxfire	3.08

Neutral (1.5 – 2.4)

Onward to Excellence	2

Summary Format

·   **Score:** Model's self-reported compatibility with service-learning based on their score on the survey.

·   **Features:** Highlights of model.

·   **Background:** When model was created, by whom it was created, and to what organization it is affiliated.

·   **Premise:** Fundamental belief that drives the model design.

·   **Design:** Description of the structure and elements of the model. This section provides insight into design components and areas correlated to service-learning.

·   **Evidence of Results:** Some information on model's impact on student achievement.

·   **Compatibility with Service-learning:** Highlights of model's compatibility with service-learning. Elements of compatibility are seen in the 12-question survey.

Assessing CSR Model's Compatibility with Service-Learning

Key elements of service-learning were incorporated into the survey (see Appendix). These are by no means the only key elements of service-learning. Many other elements exhist, but in the interest of space, the following were selected for this study.

1.   Flexible use of time, e.g., block scheduling.

Flexible use of time, in some cases, block scheduling, provides the time necessary to explore a project, or visit a community to gather data.

2.   Opportunities for students to apply their knowledge and skills, to real-life situations, problems, or projects.

The opportunity to apply classroom academic skills to a problem, situation or project within the school community or local community allows students to develop a deeper connection with the lessons they are learning. Simply providing information for students to ingest is not as powerful as allowing them the opportunity to use or apply the information in a tangible or contextual way.

3.   Address local community.

The community or school community is the partner or audience that will receive the benefit of the service-learning project or activity. Although a service-learning project or activity should be developed to help those in the community, it can also be designed to focus on the school community, such as other students, a group of teachers, or parents.

4.   Include objectives for developing civic skills and competencies.

Contributing to the common good is the essence of service-learning. The development of students' civic skills and competencies is a natural outcome of most service-learning activities and projects.

5.   Allow students to play a role in planning curricular activities.

Allowing students to be involved in designing the learning process empowers them and encourages the highest level of student interest and input. Service-learning activities and methodology engage students in the development or planning process.

6. Allow teachers to use a variety of learning materials other than textbooks.

This flexibility allows educators to reach out to other sources such as trade books, manuals, and material gathered from a class visit to a museum, animal shelter, business, community center, etc.

7. Allow teachers to use alternative teaching strategies.

Increasing the teacher's role as facilitator of learning and the use of Socratic discourse to encourage students to discuss and think through a problem are highly successful teaching strategies seen in service-learning.

8. Instructional methods include project-based learning.

Project-based learning is the instructional process that drives a service-learning activity, project, or method of teaching. Indication of this within a model's design shows strong signs of compatibility. Also, the use of applied learning or contextual learning is a promising sign of compatibility.

9. Allow teachers to use interdisciplinary team teaching and/or experiential learning methods in teaching.

Interdisciplinary team teaching aligns math, science, social studies, English language arts, and other studies around a common theme or project. Interdisciplinary teaching allows teachers to plan units of study together; bringing a sense of continuity to the student's learning experiences, a sense of connectivity.

10. Alternative assessments allowed or encouraged?

Alternative assessments such as **rubrics** provide guidelines for the level of quality in a student's work. Developing rubrics with students can enrich the learning process. When a teacher consults with students during the development of a rubric, they discuss and learn what is acceptable quality among their peers, and develop a clear understanding of what an "A" looks like. **Portfolios** allow students to showcase exceptional work through their school career. Students can store exemplary work created during a project, such as letters written to elected officials, poetry, photographs, examples of applied math, and documents written, edited and produced using computer software. **Presentations** and **projects** provide opportunities to polish skills needed in everyday life.

11. Address school or district policies regarding students' ability to leave school for outside learning activities.

School and district policies must be considered regarding students ability to leave school grounds. This was the most difficult question on the survey for school models and schools to answer.

12. Provide time for student reflection through (journal entries, classroom dialog, or discussion).

Reflection seals in the learning that happens during an activity or project. It allows teachers to discover what students know and facilitates honest discussion about what was learned, how things could have been improved, what went well, where details could have been added or deleted, and other significant insights.

ACCELERATED SCHOOLS PROJECT

University of Connecticut, Neag School of Education
2131 Hillside Road, Unit 3224, Storrs, CT 06269-3224, 860-486-6330, 860-486-6348 fax
www.acceleratedschools.net

Score: Highly Compatible

"Accelerated schools seek out, acknowledge, and build upon every child's natural curiosity, encouraging students to construct knowledge through exploration and discovery and to see connections between school activities and their lives outside the classroom."
– *Accelerated Schools Project*

Features:

◆ Set of school governance structures and principles to unify the purpose of the school.

◆ Every member of the school empowered in shared decision-making process.

◆ Talents and knowledge of every member of the school community recognized and utilized.

Background: The Accelerated Schools Project originated at Stanford University in 1986. It was designed by Henry Levin and Associates to provide a comprehensive approach to school change targeted at "At-Risk" children. The Accelerated Schools Project has moved to the Neag School of Education at the University of Connecticut, Gene Chasin, director.

Premise: All students should receive a "gifted and talented" education where they are challenged with high expectations for success. The entire school community should be engaged in the transformation of the school.

Design: Accelerated Schools Project helps schools set up priorities and governance structures to support bringing a challenging educational experience to students. The model's trademark is its strong belief that challenging learning experiences usually reserved for the 'gifted and talented' must be shared with all students. The model uses what it calls "accelerated learning" so that "both struggling learners and those who display high ability receive engaging and challenging instruction."

Accelerated Schools offers a curriculum designed to involve the community "fully." The model focuses on higher-order thinking skills and relates subject matter in the curriculum to student's lives. Students are allowed to participate in shaping their learning experience and are guided to make decisions and solve problems.

The Accelerated Schools Project has developed a set of governance and structure principles framework from a larger list of values and principles. *Unity of Purpose* is used to bring all members of the school community together to work toward a common set of goals that will benefit students. *Empowerment Coupled with Responsibility* means that every member of the school participates in a shared decision-making process, sharing in the responsibility for implementing decisions and being held accountable for the outcomes of decisions. *Building on Strengths* asks the school community to recognize and utilize the knowledge, talents, and resources of every member of the school community.

Each Accelerated School uses an internal self-assessment tool called *Tools for Assessing School Progress (TASP)*. The tool, a list of indicators, helps schools work toward demonstrating high levels of implementation of assessing school progress. The following indicators in the TASP demonstrate a strong alignment with service-learning.

- Teachers employ a variety of instructional approaches in each teaching unit and lesson.

- Teachers use resources (time, materials, classroom management, and flexible classroom organization) effectively to support student learning.

- The school and teacher provide opportunities for students to individually extend their learning and follow up on interests.

- Teachers use students' strengths and interests to plan instruction and curriculum.

- Teachers provide frequent opportunities for students to reflect, critique, revise, and extend their learning.

- Teachers include instruction assessment that is multifaceted, clear and specific, and which involves the student.

- Teachers include application to real-life situations or issues in instruction.

- Teachers include in instruction the vocabulary, methods, and/or activities in the work world or in the discipline.

- Teachers help students to demonstrate their learning through the creation of authentic products and performances.

- Students interact with the world outside the school through field-based experiences and/or technology.

- Teachers involve students in the planning of instruction.

- Instruction helps each learner to be a creator, thinker, and problem-solver.

- Teachers build the transfer of learning between one subject and another into instruction.

Evidence of Results:
In a review of CSR models in late 2001, the Education Commission of the States (ECS) found that South Carolina's network of 24 Accelerated Schools had shown increases in student achievement. Most significant were gains on the Metropolitan Achievement Test (MAT7) from 1996 to 1997 where, among second grade classes, 73 percent increased their reading scores and 55 percent increased their math scores. Increased rates of achievement for third graders were 71 percent in reading and 86 percent in math. Ninety percent of schools in the study indicated that the number of students receiving special education services was reduced, and 41 percent reported a decrease in the number of students who were retained since the adoption of the Accelerated Schools Project.

Another study by the Manpower Demonstration Research Corporation (MDRC), based on eight years of test-score data for third-graders in eight schools, found that students began to show significant gains in test scores four to five years into the program. MDRC reports that there were no positive impacts in the first two years, a slight decline in the third year as schools began to modify their curriculum and instruction, and a gradual increase in the fourth and fifth years, with "the average third-grade reading and math scores in the fifth year exceeding predicted levels by a significant amount." The researchers claim that the greatest impact was observed among students who would have scored in the middle of their school's test score distribution without the reform and among the schools that had the lowest test scores before adopting the reform. Researchers found that scores from students in schools using the Accelerated Schools Project improved despite student mobility (students moving in and out of the school system). "These findings demonstrate the potential of the Accelerated Schools approach as it was implemented early in its development, to improve student achievement," the report says. In the early days of the model's history, the practice was to first help schools develop more collaborative governance structures and then, a year or two later, turn to improving classroom instruction. Schools joining the program now, tackle both instructional and governance improvements from the start.

Compatibility with Service-Learning: The model scored as *highly compatible*.

Accelerated does not prescribe flexible use of time, leaving this matter to the school to decide. In the survey, the model referenced a design principle in their framework, "empowerment with responsibility," as a way of addressing civic skills and competencies.

Students may play a role in planning curricular activities, and student ownership for instructional decisions is embedded in the model's framework. A key element of the model, *Taking Stock*, allows students to research community resources and needs, utilizing this information to inform curriculum instruction decisions. This element is highly conducive to service-learning activities.

Although the model does not prescribe a curriculum, the framework that guides the curriculum relies on "authentic sources rather than textbooks driving instruction." Integration between subject disciplines is a core element of the model's framework. Approved assessments include portfolios, student self-evaluation, observation, and rubrics. Reflection, an essential component of service-learning is also one of the nine key values of the Accelerated Schools Project.

Two specific principles in the model design structure are highly supportive of service-learning: "Members of the community (staff, parents, community, and students) share in making decisions of importance in the school" and "Students are empowered and held responsible for extending their learning and following up in their interests."

The Accelerated Schools' *Powerful Learning Framework* integrates effective curriculum alignment, best instructional strategies, and real world context. The five components of Powerful Learning: authentic, interactive, learner-centered, inclusive, and continuous learning are closely aligned with service-learning. Accelerated's framework builds teacher capacity to deliver powerful lessons traditionally found in programs for the gifted and talented, i.e., student initiated inquiry (students asking questions), simulations, and student determined exhibitions.

Sources:
Accelerated Schools (2002). *Tools for assessing school progress (TASP)*. Retrieved 2002, from http://www.acceleratedschools.net/main_acc.htm.

Education Commission of the States (2001). *Programs and practices: A review of the Accelerated Schools Project*. Retrieved 2002, from www.ecs.org.

Manpower Demonstration Research Corporation (2001). *Evaluating the Accelerated Approach: A look at early implementation and impacts on student achievement in eight elementary schools, executive summary*. New York, NY: MDRC.

AMERICA'S CHOICE™

One Thomas Circle, Suite 700, Washington, DC 20005, 202-783-3668, 202-783-3672 fax
http://www.ncee.org

Score: Compatible

"We believe that education and training systems work best when clear standards – standards that match the highest in the world – are set for student achievement, accurate measures of progress against those standards are devised, the people closest to the students are given the authority for figuring out how to get the students to the standards and are then held accountable for student progress." – *Marc Tucker, president, National Center on Education and the Economy*

Features:

♦ *New Standards Performance Standards®*, a set of comprehensive and integrated internationally-benchmarked performance standards that specify what a student should know and be able to do by the time they reach the 4th, 8th, and 10th grades. The standards are used to guide curriculum.

♦ *Principles of Learning*, a framework for teaching and learning.

♦ Smaller learning communities, groups of 200 to 400 students. Teachers in English, math and science stay with the same group through middle or lower high school.

♦ Catch-up literacy and math programs, and intensive middle and high school courses to bring new students up to the standards.

♦ Safety nets for students at risk of dropping out.

♦ School-to-work partnership program and career academy options.

♦ Multiple types of assessments including rubrics, portfolios, and the *New Standards Reference Exam®* linked to standards.

♦ *America's Choice Network* to share learning among practitioners.

Background: America's Choice was created in 1997 and evolved from work done in the 1990s by the National Alliance For Restructuring Education (NARE), a project of the National Center on Education and the Economy (NCEE).

Premise: An expectation to do whatever it takes to make sure that all but the most severely handicapped students achieve standards in English language arts (ELA), math and science, and graduate from high school qualified to do college-level work without remediation.

Design: America's Choice covers preschool through grade 12. The model breaks large high schools into a lower division (9th and 10th grades) and an upper division (11th and 12th). In the high school years, the design's strategy is for all students to reach the 10th grade performance standards in ELA and mathematics before they graduate. Courses are sequenced, focusing on basic skills and knowledge in core disciplines, conceptual development, and problem solving to help students meet the standards.

Some of the model's *Principles of Learning* are highly compatible with service-learning. These include:

• Students need a thinking curriculum–one that provides deep understanding of the subject and the ability to apply that understanding to the complex, real-world problems students will face as an adult.

• Students of all ages learn best in two types of circumstances: when they are seeking and using knowledge and skills to address problems that challenge and engage them and when they are teaching others.

• People learn well when working beside an expert who models skilled practice and encourages and guides learners as they create products or performances for audiences whose reaction really matters.

The America's Choice ELA program for high school, also called the "100-day curriculum," is geared to prepare students in English classes to reach the standards. In an effort to meet the needs of all students, including those entering the classroom with limited English skills, the America's Choice model includes a double period of English in the freshman year. English teachers who teach the double period attend seminars and use classroom sets of leveled texts to move the students to higher achievement levels. Leveled books are a key component in a guided reading program. Guided reading is an approach to the teaching of reading that uses small group instruction and developmentally appropriate books.

The America's Choice mathematics program supplements and strengthens regular math coursework so that students learn problem solving and basic skills and gain a deep understanding of mathematics concepts. Student who have not met the standard in mathematics are assigned to a special course called Fundamentals of Mathematics. This course is designed to deliver higher levels of mathematics to students who are far below grade level. Students who have failed to meet the standards in both subjects participate in both programs.

The model's strategy for measuring results is called *Planning for Results*. This system guides the implementation of the design within the school and measures academic progress of students. The America's Choice management system requires constant analysis of student performance data and ongoing adjustment of the program to meet student needs.

America's Choice schools are encouraged to communicate regularly with parents about student progress and to engage the school and community in understanding how the standards work and what role parents play in school improvement. The *Community Supports and Services* component within the model coordinates all related programs and services of the community, such as local social service and public health agencies on behalf of the students in the schools. The model helps the School Leadership Team develop a public engagement program for parents and interested members of the community to provide them with a voice in school affairs, enabling the school to communicate well with its constituencies, and broaden and deepen community support for the reform program.

Evidence of Results: A five-year study of America's Choice is being conducted by the Center for Policy Research in Education (CPRE), *Moving Mountains: The Successes and Challenges of America's Choice*. The report reveals statistically significant increases of two to six percent in student achievement in reading and math by students in America's Choice schools versus those in the study's control group. There is also some evidence that although the early stages of America's Choice implementation focuses mainly on literacy, some positive effect on students' mathematics performance can be seen. For example, increasing students' ability to read allowed them to more clearly read word problems and test instructions. The study also reveals that incorporating the use of standards in a school setting is not easy and takes time and dedication as well as strong support from the school district.

ELA teachers reported in the CPRE study that after implementation of the model, their classrooms were more structured and organized. Teacher observations included: "I am now more focused on writing across all subject areas," and "My teaching is now more focused on using the standards to guide my instruction." Incorporating American's Choice design elements into the classroom takes a considerable amount of work by the teacher, but dedication to the design helps improve academic instruction. One teacher commented , "I stopped trying to get 27 papers that looked the same. The result was that students have ownership of their writing and the topics they select." Other teachers affirmed that students were becoming more responsible for their learning, thus creating different work for educators.

Compatibility with Service-Learning: America's Choice scored itself as *compatible* with service-learning. Compatible activities include, for example, high school students are expected to participate in a peer-tutoring program to read to elementary students. Peer tutoring is a common service-learning activity. Guided by the model's applied learning standards, students prepare oral presentations of project plans concerning community issues to present to local councils and businesses . Schools surveyed suggest that any of the model's applied learning standards would correlate with objectives for developing civic skills and competencies. Through training in the model's *Standards-Driven Curriculum: Course One*, teachers create units of study that engage students in authentic assessments connected to real-life situations.

The model supports the involvement of students in the creation and interpretation of rubrics for assessment purposes, another area of compatibility with service-learning. "In reading and writing, students make choices about what they read and write and how they demonstrate their knowledge and skills," wrote the developer. Schools surveyed report student involvement in this capacity writing, "Students are slowly becoming involved in the planning process," and "Students network to solve problems."

America's Choice allows teachers to use a variety of learning materials beyond traditional textbooks. Schools say they are using the Internet as a source, exploring with author studies, genre studies, and inviting guest presenters who bring their own materials. "Teachers are using assorted materials. We are buying fewer books than in the past. This is a good sign," wrote one school. Teachers are also working together in teams. "We establish in larger schools 'Houses' and interdisciplinary teams for planning and instruction that crosses disciplines," wrote another school.

The model is supportive of schools whose teachers wish to use alternative teaching strategies suggesting, "While we try to help teachers increase their instructional strategies by teaching them to use 'guided reading,' etc., they can draw on their own 'bag of tricks' and add to it." This kind of flexibility suggests that America's Choice accommodates a teacher's choice to introduce service-learning (linked to standards). Schools said that less lecture was being used and that group work was becoming much more dominant in the classroom. Terms such as "mapping," "boggle techniques," and "popcorn sessions with student discovery" are used. One school wrote that the America's Choice Core Assignments in ELA "promote strategies that give students experience in observing, recording and interviewing people."

The model offers some instructional methods that include project-based learning. Senior projects focus on project-based learning and integrate applied learning standards into project-based learning. One America's Choice school wrote that teachers are using project-based group activities as an application to help their students make real-life connections.

The model is concerned with preparing students to enter the world after high school writing, "We have at the high school level requirements for an Academic Foundation Certificate that requires students to complete a portfolio project. Our applied learning performance standards are aligned with [the U.S. Department of Labor's] SCANS Report and aim to build skills and competencies that prepare students for the world of work."

Alternative assessments such as portfolios and rubrics are supported by America's Choice. Schools surveyed wrote that structured reflection was built into activities such as journal writing, end-of-period reflection on daily lessons, and a readers/writers workshop.

The America's Choice model's standards-driven curriculum provides a strong base on which to weave service-learning. The model links to the New Standards Performance Standards® which include, along with English, math and science standards, a substantial list of applied learning standards that align smoothly with service-learning. Examples in the high school version of the applied learning standards include:

Problem Solving: The student conducts projects involving at least two of the following kinds of problem solving each year and, over the course of high school, conducts projects involving all three kinds of problem solving.

- Design a Product, Service, or System: Identify needs that could be met by new products, services, or systems and create solutions for meeting them.

- Improve a System: Develop an understanding of the way systems of people, machines, and processes work; troubleshoot problems in their operation and devise strategies for improving their effectiveness.

- Plan and Organize an Event or Activity: Take responsibility for all aspects of planning and organizing an event or activity from concept to completion, making good use of the resources of people, time, money, materials and facilities.

Service-learning could be introduced in a lesson plan produced through the model's *Standards-Driven Curriculum: Course I*, but service-learning is not directly addressed by the model even through its applied learning standards. Schools incorporating America's Choice must either have a service-learning culture within the school, or a strong service-learning leader within the school to ensure it is not lost within the model's design.

Sources:
Education Commission of the States (2001). *Programs and practices: A review of the America's Choice Network.* Retrieved 2002, from www.ecs.org.

National Center on Education and the Economy, Home page http://www.ncee.org/.

Supovitz, J. A., Poglinco, S. M., and Snyder, B.A. (2001). *Moving mountains: Successes and challenges of the America's Choice comprehensive school reform design.* Philadelphia, PA: Consortium for Policy Research in Education.

ATLAS COMMUNITIES

55 Chapel Street, Newton, MA 02158-1060, 617-969-7100, 617-969-3440 fax
http://www.atlascommunities.org

Score: Compatible

"If children receive this message consistently, if they learn the skills and habits that reinforce their own talents and interests, if teachers are engaged in their own learning, if families and communities are involved in the daily life of the school, if the school and pathway are organized around the demands of the disciplines, as well as other forms of mastery ... then our children will come to see themselves as citizens long before they step out into the workforce and the world at large."
– ATLAS Communities

Features:

♦ *Pathways*–Partnership between Pre-K, elementary, middle, and high schools to provide continuity for students and their families.

♦ Organizational structures that enhance communication, keeping all stakeholders in the ATLAS Communities sites informed and engaged in the restructuring process.

♦ Faculty members encouraged to design authentic (real-life) curricular and assessment strategies that give students a chance to apply what they have learned to real-world situations.

♦ Teachers meet regularly in study groups dedicated to improving instructional practice.

Background: ATLAS Communities is housed at Education Development Center, Inc., Newton, Massachusetts. ATLAS Communities was founded in 1992 by James Comer of the School Development Program at Yale University, Howard Gardner of Project Zero at Harvard University, Theodore Sizer of the Coalition of Essential Schools at Brown University, and Janet Whitla of Education Development Center in Newton, Massachusetts.

Premise: ATLAS Communities fosters teachers who are committed to improving their practice, administrators who believe all students can learn, parents who expect the most from their children's schools and are actively engaged in their education, community members who feel proud of their school, and students who "deserve the best education possible."

A Pre-K-12 pathway is essential to improving learning outcomes for all students. Planning, research, action, and reflection are seen as the backbone of effective teaching, learning, and organizational change. Authentic curriculum, instruction, and assessment are critical to challenge students and engage them in "purposeful work." Relationship building is respected as "an important social learning activity." Parent engagement is seen as crucial to student achievement.

Design: The model links Pre-K, elementary, middle, and high schools together in one "pathway" as partners in creating consistent, personalized education where all children achieve. This feeder pattern enables schools to work together to provide a seamless school experience for every student.

The model works with sites for three to five years with an ATLAS site developer to create coherent pathways. Teachers and administration from each grade level form teams to ensure a smooth progression from one grade to the next. The site developer provides customized technical assistance, and other ATLAS specialists provide on-site, telephone, and online consultation related to professional development, curriculum, and assessment. A Pathway Leadership Team is developed at the school to provide stewardship for the school revitalization effort. The Team is guided by the model to do research, data analysis, and planning with other schools in their pathway. The site developer helps schools develop a strategy for clear communication with all stakeholders during the restructuring process and to search for potential funding sources.

ATLAS Communities provides teachers with a process for developing assessment methods and curricula that are aligned with state standards. All teachers are asked to participate in an ongoing study group that examines instructional practice. Teachers review research on teaching methods and use evaluation data, including authentic assessments developed by the school, to evaluate their own practices in relation to student learning and to set the reform agenda for the coming school year. Teachers attend professional development institutes at Project Zero, an educational research group at the Harvard Graduate School of Education, where they explore effective instructional practices, technology integration, and literacy development. This affords teachers the time to meet, learn, and create lesson plans. ATLAS schools combine assessments such as portfolios with student exhibitions to get a more comprehensive view of student achievement.

Family and community involvement is included in the model design. In one ATLAS school in Seattle, a VISTA volunteer was included in the Pathway Family and Community Team to help plan and implement an Earth Day activity, helping students develop a "deep understanding of essential concepts, habits, and skills needed for productive work and informed citizenry." At an elementary school in Philadelphia, student-led tours through the surrounding neighborhood identified the assets of the community, which in turn provided the content for authentic classroom projects and exhibitions tied to state and local standards. The model views the community as an asset to the education of students and fundamental to the long-term sustainability of school improvement efforts.

Evidence of Results: The implementation of the ATLAS framework in schools has led to improvements in school culture and significant changes in instructional methods, student work,

and involvement of parents and members of the community in school activities. Based on data reported by ATLAS schools and their districts, standardized test scores have increased in all pathways that have worked with the ATLAS framework for three years or more.

At Tanners Creek Elementary in Norfolk, Virginia, the percentage of fifth grade students passing a literacy pretest increased more in reading and writing than district-wide averages between 1992 and 1996. In reading, passing scores increased from 78.4 percent in 1992 to 85 percent in 1996, and math scores increased from 72.7 percent to 88 percent, respectively. District-wide scores in reading increased from 72.2 percent passing in 1992 to 77 percent in 1996, and in math from 72.4 percent to 75 percent, respectively.

The Woodinville Pathway in Northshore, Washington exhibited solid upward trends in reading and math at the elementary and middle school level since the implementation of ATLAS in September 1997. Woodin Elementary, once the lowest performing school in the district, increased its scores significantly in reading and math between 1997 and 2000. In reading, the percentage of students meeting standards rose from 60.3 percent in 1997 to 73.2 percent in 2000. In 1997, less than half (30.7 percent) of Leota Junior High School students met the math standards, but by 2000, 53.5 percent met or exceeded the standards.

One cluster of ATLAS schools in Philadelphia, Pennsylvania exceeded performance targets set by the district to measure improvement after two years of implementing ATLAS between 1996 and 1998.

According to the North Central Regional Education Laboratory's (NCREL) review of ATLAS in their study guide of CSR models, standardized test scores have increased in all pathways that have worked with ATLAS communities for three years or more. Elementary reading scores on the Comprehensive Test of Basic Skills (CTBS) in Prince George's County, Maryland raised an average of 13 percent in two years, and an increase of 15 percent was seen in Norfolk, Virginia on the Test for Achievement Proficiency for reading, writing, and science among scores from 11th grade students. Schools using the model also report that discipline problems and drop-out rates have decreased.

Compatibility with Service-Learning: The model scored itself as *compatible* with service-learning, however, after closer analysis, it is clear that the model is *highly compatible*. On the survey, the model scored nine key service-learning elements as being "highly compatible" with its design. Areas that demonstrate this high compatibility are where the model encourages: project-based learning, which relies heavily on flexible use of time and interdisciplinary learning; flexibility among varied learning materials beyond traditional textbooks; alternative teaching strategies, including those used in the multiple intelligence theory; and assessments such as portfolios, exhibitions, and performance. The model encourages teachers to meet in faculty study groups to look at student data and to work with other teachers to improve their teaching techniques. This, according to ATLAS, leads to increased interdisciplinary and experiential strategies.

There are a number of areas where service-learning could be integrated into the design. The model features authentic curriculum, instruction, and assessment. Service-learning epitomizes authentic learning. Service-learning also helps fuel students' ideas for exhibition and portfolio work. It also fosters greater contact with the community, an integral component to ATLAS Communities' school restructuring process.

Sources:

ATLAS Communities Information Packet 2000. Retrieved 2002, from www.atlascommunities.org.

North Central Regional Educational Laboratory (2000). *Comprehensive school reform models: A study guide for comparing CSR models (and how well they meet Minnesota's learning standards)*. Retrieved 2002, from http://www.ncrel.org/csri/respub/models/intro.htm.

Northwest Regional Educational Laboratory (2001). The catalog of school reform models. Retrieved 2002, from http://www.nwrel.org/scpd/catalog/index.shtml.

Seattle Public Schools (2000). *Beacon Hill ATLAS Pathway: Year end report*. Seattle, WA: Author. Retrieved 2002, from http://www.blarg.net/~building/restr_atlas.htm.

AUDREY COHEN COLLEGE:

Purpose-Centered Education® K-12, 75 Varick Street,New York, NY 10013-1919
212-343-1234, ext. 3400, 212-343-8472 fax
http://www.audrey-cohen.edu

Score: Highly Compatible

"Purpose-Centered Education links education and life. It brings the classroom into the community and the community into the classroom." – *Audrey Cohen*

Features:

♦ *Purpose-Centered Education®*
♦ *Purpose-Achievement Standards®*
♦ *Constructive Action®*

Background: In 1970, educator Audrey Cohen and her colleagues developed Purpose-Centered Education System spanning kindergarten through postsecondary education. Cohen, in *Phi Delta Kappan* 1993, discussed the basis for the Audrey Cohen College approach to school reform.

Premise: The answer to better education for students lies in correcting the traditional approach to education that focuses on accumulating the knowledge of the ages and concentrates on teaching children the answers to other people's questions. The Audrey Cohen College school model seeks to develop a sophisticated, holistic and performance-based approach that focuses on challenges that will generate and support students' search for knowledge. This trans-disciplinary system seeks to "organize learning around purposes that motivate children to find answers."

Design: Audrey Cohen's respect for student involvement in the community lives in *Purpose-Centered Education*. "Too often today, the classroom remains separate from the larger world. As a result, students do not have the opportunity to address real challenges. They learn skills that have little application to their future." *Purpose-Centered Education* seeks to change this by making academic learning purposeful learning, encouraging students to use their knowledge to make a positive contribution

to our world. For example, a class may apply its academic learning to a broad "theme" of social issues to answer questions like, "How can we improve education while effectively meeting the needs of an expanding global society?" The model trains schools to link knowledge to action within the local and world community, achieving meaningful goals, while aiming for high academic standards and developing student knowledge of core subject matter. *Purpose-Centered Education* motivates students to become deeply involved in their own education. Audrey Cohen College Schools expect students to become great thinkers, problem solvers, model leaders, and scholars.

According to Janith Jordan, Vice President of Audrey Cohen College Schools, the model prepares children and youth for postsecondary education, challenging careers, and thoughtful civic participation. It nurtures in students an appreciation for their ability to affect the world they live in, and the larger world they are about to enter, and helps to build a desire within students for lifelong learning. Students are taught to use what they have learned in their core subjects to reach specific goals. Classes are coordinated so that a Purpose, such as "We Develop School-Business Partnerships" streams, is integrated, through all core subject areas. Throughout the grade levels, students use technology as a research and communication tool in achieving their purpose. PCE is used by students in rural, suburban, and urban schools, and works equally well with gifted, at-risk, immigrant, and students with special needs.

The College's model gives each grade level from K-12 a specific Purpose appropriate to the age of the students. Each grade level through the ninth grade is given two Purposes, one for the first semester and one for the second, serving to integrate English language arts, mathematics, science, and social studies core curriculum for that time. For example, in the fourth grade first semester the Purpose is "We Work for Good Health." During this time, all subjects will focus on this overarching Purpose, or theme. For the second semester, the Purpose is "We Use Inventions to Make Life Better." Starting in grade seven, the Purpose curriculum changes from "We" to "I." As the grades increase towards high school there is a shift toward Purposes that prepare students for postsecondary education and civic responsibility. From grade ten on, one Purpose flows through the entire year. For example, the tenth-grade core curriculum is driven by the Purpose "I Use Science and Technology to Help Shape a Just and Productive Society."

Audrey Cohen College has also developed *Purpose-Achievement Standards*® (PAS). Research conducted by the college assesses the attributes of highly successful adults, revealing that successful people are "very purposeful in their actions." Twenty-four "generic abilities" were identified from the research and were modified into what the College calls Purpose-Achievement. Examples of PAS include:

- Select a worthwhile and feasible goal for action.

- Develop a plan of action.

- Express ethical principles and reasoning in actions aimed at achieving your purpose.

- Initiate and maintain effective interpersonal relationships.

Taking Constructive Action® refers to the concept of achieving a Purpose in the community. This is the underpinning of the Audrey Cohen College school design, and provides the method by which knowledge is linked with action. It also serves as a guide for assessing how students have used knowledge to make a positive impact outside the classroom. Constructive Action has three phases: planning, implementation and assessment. Students decide the goal for their Constructive Action, with guidance from the teacher, and use English, history, math, science, and geography to pursue their Purpose. An example given by the model describes ninth-graders in a Florida high school who are addressing adolescent health problems. Students conducted a survey to identify problems that most concerned their peers, and based on the survey results, arranged for a series of speakers to address these health issues. The students also visited a health center at a neighborhood college and prepared a proposal for a school-based health center for their high school. Their plan included a budget and model of their solution to the problem. Students took the plan to school authorities for approval for the Center went forward. Although the College does not specifically use the term to describe a problem solving project like this, some would clearly identify it as service-learning.

Another focus of the Audrey Cohen College model is *Values and Ethics*. Through complex and thought-provoking questions such as, "How do I learn to appreciate and balance the competing interests and values of different people in my family and in the organizations I am part of?" and, "What do responsibility and integrity require of me?" Students grow on an intellectual level and begin to develop negotiating skills that will help them navigate successfully through life. The model believes that as soon as schools begin to relate academic learning to Purpose and Constructive Action, they begin to expand the scope of what students can learn, not only from academic material, but from competencies to which academic material will be applied.

The model's *Dimensions of Learning, Action and Assessment*® is the name for curriculum that specifically coordinates a broad range of core subject knowledge and basic skills that students must know in order to achieve their purposes. Dimension classes create an environment for a rigorous learning experience. Dimension integrates core subject knowledge and skills with relevance and action. The five Dimensions are: Purpose, Values and Ethics, Self and Others, Systems, and Skills. For example, students "synthesize knowledge developed though other Dimensions classes. They assess their success in achieving Purpose and their effectiveness in using knowledge as a basis for action, implementing the Constructive Action in the community and larger world."

Evidence of Results: The Alabama Department of Education and the Office of the Superintendent, Montgomery Public Schools released test results on the model. On the Stanford Achievement Test in 1999/00, after one year using the Purpose-Centered Education model, grade 3 student scores in reading increased by 72 percent, grade 4 student scores increased by 56 percent, and grade 5 student scores also increased by 56 percent at Peterson Elementary Classical Grammar School. In mathematics, grade 3 student scores increased by 119 percent, grade 4 increased by 66 percent, and grade 5 by 82 percent. Parental involvement at the school during the year increased by 285 percent, from 972 parents to 3,749 parents. Sumter County High School in York, Alabama registered sizeable gains on the annual SAT for the same year. After one year of implementation of the model, scores in mathematics increased in grade 9 by 10 percent. In grade 10, scores increased by 74 percent, and in grade 11 by 52 percent. Language scores were also significantly increased.

According to Janith Jordan, positive indicators of the model's success include improvements in standardized test scores in reading, mathematics, and language; increased school attendance and decreased discipline problems; and supportive parental reactions to the model. With the model's design implemented, "students see a reason to learn."

Compatibility with Service-Learning: The model scored itself as *highly compatible* with service-learning. Although the developer did not wish the model to be associated with the term service-learning, because they have developed

their own term for it–Purpose-Centered Education®, the elements of the design, for all intents and purposes, would be recognized as service-learning. Not only does the model integrate its core curriculum and align it with state standards, it promotes the use of the community as a focus for learning. The model also integrates core curriculum components with skills such as negotiating, critical thinking, problem solving, communication and research to help students apply their academic knowledge to community problems.

The model's Purposed-Centered curriculum has several key components that can be addressed in different combinations each week, allowing educators flexible use of time for teaching. The curriculum is organized around Dimensions of Learning, Action, and Assessment: Purpose, Values and Ethics, Self and Others, Systems and Skills. The Purpose-Centered curriculum brings students into the community to achieve their Purpose every semester. Students must demonstrate through their academic achievement that they have improved their community. Students also follow *Constructive Action*, a methodology developed by the college, to enhance leadership skills.

Purpose-Centered Education supports student-directed learning where students become active partners in the planning of their learning experiences. Students learn in groups, and make educational decisions together as they work to achieve their Purpose and acquire knowledge from core subjects. Students and teachers use a variety of resources, such as books, meetings with professionals and leaders in the community, and the Internet.

Students develop a Purpose Achiever® portfolio that provides evidence that they have used core subjects to achieve the semester's Purpose. Students keep journals to document their progress when they have met the standards, and formally reflect on their accomplishments each semester.

Sources:

Audrey Cohen College (1998). *Purpose-Centered Education: Meeting tomorrow's standards for leadership and scholarship today*. New York, NY.

Audrey Cohen College (2000, November). *A summary of the signs of success in the three Alabama Public Schools implementing Purpose-Centered Education*. New York, NY.

Blair, J. (1998, October 28). A gift of good fortune. *Education Week*, *18* (9), 32-37.

Cohen, A. (1993). A new educational paradigm. *Phi Delta Kappan, 74*, 791-795.

CENTER FOR EFFECTIVE SCHOOLS

College of Continuing Education, 555 Constitution Street, Suite 211, Norman, OK 73072
405-325-7080, 405-325-1981 fax
http://tel.occe.ou.edu/main/welcome/effective.html

Score: Compatible

"The characteristics of Effective Schools, referred to as 'the correlates,' were never intended as a prescription, recipe, or checklist. The correlates are characteristics that seem to be associated with higher student achievement and other indicators of school and student success."
– *Barbara O. Taylor and Pamela Bullard*

Features:

♦ A framework for increased student performance and teacher effectiveness, called *Seven Correlates of Effectiveness*.

♦ High impact, capacity-building training, and technical assistance that leads to Learner-Centered School Improvement.

♦ Authentic curriculum compatible with W. Edward Deming's principles of Total Quality Management (TQM).

Background: The model was developed beginning in 1986 by Beverly Bancroft, Larry Lezotte, and Barbara Taylor at Michigan State University. Larry Lezotte has formed a separate organization of a similar name, called Effective Schools Products, based on the Center for Effective Schools model.

Elements of the Center for Effective Schools (CES) design were articulated in 1977 in Pontiac, Michigan as an amalgamation of three demonstration projects (Pontiac Project, School Improvement Project, and Rising to Individual Scholastic Excellence). In the early 1980's the Effective Schools movement produced research called "All Children Can Learn." With the support of then Secretary of Education William Bennett, the design's *Seven Correlates of Effectiveness* became expanded descriptions of "what works" in school reform.

Premise: All children can master the basic skills needed to be successful in school. True equity in education can be achieved only when classroom teachers are trained and held accountable for teaching all students.

Design: The model developers refer to their design as a change process, or rather, the Effective Schools Process that can be used at all levels of education to restructure and reorganize schools, districts, and even state boards of education to focus on the goal that all children will learn the intended curriculum to a high standard. According to the developers, the Effective Schools Process complements new pedagogical strategies, such as cooperative learning, mastery learning, the Comer Process, Essential Schools curriculum development, Accelerated Schools, Comprehension and Cognition, and other curriculum initiatives.

The model is based on *Seven Correlates of Effectiveness*:

1. Instructional leadership.

2. Clearly stated and focused mission.

3. Safe and orderly environment.

4. Frequent monitoring of teacher and student progress.

5. High expectations for all students.

6. Maximize learning opportunities.

7. Positive communication between the school, home, and community.

The Effective Schools Process may be introduced into a school or district at varied entry points depending on the school's culture or the district's present organization and attitude about the level of change needed. Center for Essential

Schools staff work with the school or district to set their mission, goals, and objectives, and to build a strategic plan to be "prioritized, planned, implemented, evaluated, and refined in a cycle that repeats over two or three years."

The Effective Schools Process is formulated by those most directly affected by school reform, namely, the teaching staff, principal, support staff, and district staff. The process is approved or rejected by the school board with parents playing a large part in helping to identify priorities in the school's action plan and helping school staff carry out the process of reform.

The model adapts to a school or district's interest in implementing a particular classroom method, such as cooperative learning and sets the Effective Schools Process in motion with that design in mind. For example, if teachers who are trained in the process of cooperative learning need help implementing a schedule that allows them to have longer class periods, CES staff will help them develop channels of communication at the school and district level to secure waivers of policies and requirements to accomplish their goals. Cooperative learning involves deliberately structuring working groups of students so that they reflect the population of the classroom. Students learn from each other, build greater understanding of differences and similarities, and increase tolerance while learning to value diversity.

A professional development module called *School-Based Instructional Leadership* (SBIL) breaks down barriers in communication between the classroom, schools, and the district The module focuses on: shared decision making, school-based management, strategic planning, data collection, team building, conflict resolution, and other "skill" areas that enable faculty to use time effectively.

The model's professional development process creates and manages solid organizational transformation throughout the school or district. The process is designed around the following points.

1. Develop skills and attitudes for shared leadership on school improvement teams.

2. Synthesize, coordinate, and integrate otherwise fragmented efforts around a common framework that focuses on student learning.

3. Build internal capacity for dissemination and follow-up.

4. Provide a readiness base for more ambitious or extensive restructuring efforts.

5. Encourage collaboration among school improvement facilitators.

6. Other components:
   - District Leadership Overview
   - Effective Schools Profile Survey
   - School Leadership Academy
   - School Improvement Team
   - Teacher Professional Development
   - Internal Coaches Training
   - External Coaches
   - On-Site Visits
   - On-Site Training
   - Newsletter
   - Annual Progress and Evaluation Report

Evidence of Results: No current third-party evaluations of the model were found. However, researchers of the Effective Schools Process from the Center for Educational Leadership Services at Kent State University developed what they call the Instructional Design process to help schools and districts restructure the delivery and assessment of instruction and to monitor the impact on student achievement. Between 1997 and 2000, the Center conducted a three-year, six district demonstration project based on their Instructional Design process. This process was piloted in districts whose school boards had adopted the Effective Schools Process. During the project, districts linked national and state content standards to academic performance indictors, developed yearlong curriculum maps for each subject and grade level, and devised unit plans to guide the delivery and assessment of classroom instruction, specifying teaching and assessment techniques aligned with unit objectives. Two of the districts incorporated an electronic data management system to monitor student mastery.

At the end of the three-year demonstration project, researchers documented outcomes and improvements, including gains in the competence of teachers, a teacher's perception of his or her own competence, and effects on student mastery of performance indicators. Interviews with teachers revealed that the introduction of the project along with influence from the model brought:

- greater attention to problem-solving and other challenging activities in classrooms and less time spent on memory-level work and busywork;

- improved alignment of expected outcomes, teaching strategies, and assessments;

- better connections between subject areas as a result of curriculum mapping;

- greater variety in teaching methods, for example: inquiry, guided discussion, action research;

- more authentic performance assessments; and

- an opportunity for teachers to collaborate with teachers at the same grade level as well as those above and below.

Compatibility with Service-Learning: The model ranked itself as *compatible* with service-learning. One of the model's seven correlates focuses on parent and community communication and involvement. Although CES sees the importance of including the community as a stakeholder, it does not make significant overtures to encourage the engagement of the community in the school's curriculum.

The model supports involvement of students in the planning and decision-making process for curriculum. One school comment supported this, "The model allows students to be part of the planning process." The respondent admitted that this was not currently being explored at the school.

The model posits that there is more than one strategy to teach the curriculum. "The teacher's guide is the state standards, and teaching strategies are determined by the students' and teacher's aptitude." A CES school agreed that teachers use trade books, videos, and supplementary materials if they wish. "Teachers can use instructional strategies like direct instruction, cooperative grouping, small group instruction, flex groupings and more." The model is flexible to a school or district's interest in implementing a specific classroom teaching methodology. Service-learning, then, if chosen, could be incorporated into the Effective Schools Process.

The concept of integrated teaching and learning is actively promoted by the Effective Schools Process and helps to make educational experiences more coherent and meaningful to students. The model is neutral to experimentation with new methods of teaching and sees it as something that should be addressed if this is the will of the teachers and other stakeholders.

Alternative assessments that allow educators to frequently monitor student progress, such as portfolios, are included in the model's seven correlates. The model does not directly address the concept of providing time for student reflection, but this is not ruled out or forbidden.

Sources:

Harwell, S. H., & Blank, W. E. (2001). *Promising practices for contextual learning*, Waco, TX: CCI Publishing, p. 66.

March, J. K., & Peters, K. H. (2002). Curriculum development and instructional design in the Effective Schools Process. *Phi Delta Kappan, 83*(5), 379-381.

North Central Regional Educational Laboratory (2000). *Comprehensive School Reform models: A study guide for comparing CSR Models (and how well they meet Minnesota's Learning Standards)*. Retrieved 2002, from http://www.ncrel.org/csri/respub/models/index.html.

Taylor, B. O. (2002). The Effective Schools Process: Alive and well. *Phi Delta Kappan, 83* (5), 375-378.

Taylor, B.O. & Bullard, P. (1995). *The revolution revisited: Effective schools and systemic reform*. Bloomington, Indiana: Phi Delta Kappan Educational Foundation.

COALITION OF ESSENTIAL SCHOOLS

1814 Franklin Street, Suite 700, Oakland CA, 94612, 510-433-1915, 510-433-1455 fax
http://www.essentialschools.org

Score: Highly Compatible

"Around the nation, more people are asking whether schools as most now look—large, anonymous places that shuttle students through a fragmented day and test them with impersonal zeal—are designed to best yield the engaged and thoughtful citizens the next century requires."
– *Coalition of Essential Schools*

Features:

♦ *Ten Common Principles* guide school practice and priorities.

♦ Professional Development program through Coalition University.

♦ Building an ethos of community.

♦ Network of Coalition schools.

♦ Teacher's role as facilitator.

Background: Theodore (Ted) Sizer of Brown University founded the model beginning in 1984. He then created the Coalition in an attempt to address problems with secondary schools as identified in a five-year study, chaired by him, that revealed unfulfilling educational experiences for students, consisting of lectures and drills, with little opportunity provided to think deeply about important issues or to produce meaningful work. The Coalition has become a national network of schools and centers engaged in restructuring schools to promote better student learning. Sizer also provided input into the Paideia model design (listed later in this study).

Premise: Provide better teaching and genuine learning for American high schools. Allow teachers to serve as facilitators to promote student inquiry and development of skills.

Design: The Coalition's school model is based upon *Ten Common Principles*:

1. Learning to use one's mind well.

2. Less is more.

3. Depth over knowledge.

4. School's goals should apply to all students.

5. Personalization.

6. Student as worker and teacher as coach.

7. Demonstration of mastery in exhibition.

8. Tone of decency and trust.

9. Teacher as generalist.

10. Student-centered administrative choices, democracy and equity.

The Coalition uses the Principles to inspire a school to examine its priorities in school design, classroom practice, leadership, and community connections. The model provides support for this work by providing: professional development, conducting research, and fostering a network of communication among Coalition schools.

Classroom practice is guided by key ideas put forth by the model. The Coalition believes the teacher's role is to be a facilitator to promote student inquiry and development of skills. The curriculum should be deep and thorough with the aim of developing an inquisitive mind, multiple perspectives, and applying learning to new situations. The curriculum should also be flexible and individualized to allow for independent exploration. Students who do not meet standards should be given intensive support. Teachers should be afforded plentiful professional learning opportunities and should be allowed to network to build upon each others knowledge. The model offers schools specific support including coaching for teacher collaboration and inquiry, site visits to other "like-minded schools," peer coaching training, and Coalition University courses on instruction.

For school leaders, the Coalition's program demands both high quality formal leadership and collaboration with others in the school community. School leaders are expected to provide support for ongoing improvement in instructional practices and to keep the school on track with reform efforts. Decision-making procedures should be done in a democratic manner and should communicate a tone of high expectations, trust, and decency. Teachers are considered to be school leaders and should have authority over their work and time for collaboration. The model provides professional development and coaching with principal institutes, school leadership institutes, cross-school collaboration groups, leadership team meetings, and Coalition University courses on topics such as instructional leadership and resource allocation.

The model developer believes that family and community should be involved in the intellectual development of students. The model is guided by the idea that student learning should be tied to the community and the world outside the school. This allows students to do much of their learning outside of school walls and under the guidance of mentors from the community. Community partnerships are key. The model supports this belief by providing facilitation of community engagement events, facilitation of school-community partnerships and Coalition University courses that help to build community alliances, and using the community as a classroom.

Evidence of Results: Central Park East Secondary School in East Harlem, New York has seen 90 percent of their ninth graders graduate compared with 55 percent citywide. Ninety percent of those graduating also go on to attend college. A Macmullen study in 1996 showed evidence suggesting that two key approaches used by the Coalition of Essential Schools,

"authentic pedagogy" and "sense of community," can lead to higher student achievement.

The Muncey and McQullen study of 1996 revealed that it is difficult to put the design's Principles into practice in comprehensive high schools. These studies agree that selected teachers make profound changes in classroom practice.

According to Kathy Simon, Director of Research at the Coalition of Essential Schools, a study by educators/researchers Darling-Hammond, Ancess, and Ort, to be published in a forthcoming edition of the *American Educational Research Journal* (2002) reveals promising results for the model. The study shows that students in the five Coalition Campus Schools in New York City Schools, formed as small schools after the closing of Julia Richman High School, graduate at a higher rate than those in similar schools. Students also drop out less frequently and are more likely to go on to college. In 1997, 86 percent of the first graduating class went on to college and in 1998, 91 percent of the second graduating class went on to college.

Compatibility with Service-Learning: The model scored itself as *highly compatible* with service-learning. The model encourages flexible and in-depth learning experiences through the use of extended blocks of time or class periods that vary in relation to the needs of the students' inquiry (some schools have up to 120 minutes or whole mornings in their blocks).

The Coalition model also encourages real-life application of knowledge and skills through Principle 6–Demonstration of mastery in exhibition: "Teaching and learning should be documented and assessed with tools based on student performance of real tasks. Multiple forms of evidence, ranging from ongoing observation of the learner to completion of specific projects should be used to understand the student's strengths and needs and to plan for further assistance. Students should have opportunities to exhibit their expertise before family and community. The diploma should be awarded upon a successful final demonstration of mastery for graduation–an 'Exhibition.'" In response to the survey question on flexible time in school, one Coalition school wrote, "We have a 'Week Without Walls' program and advisory staff are challenged to create relevant curriculum."

Local community needs are addressed by the model. Community Connections is a focus area created to develop and sustain meaningful interactive relationships with a school's community (parents, education, civic, business) so that all members become familiar with and support the work of the school. Project-based learning and outside learning activities are supported and encouraged by the Coalition process, allowing students to leave the school and pursue learning activities in their local communities and beyond. "Authentic application is an essential part of our program," wrote one school.

The curriculum supported by the model includes development of civic responsibilities. "[The Coaltion] strongly believes in developing a tone of decency within the school community, as well as pushing its students to think deeply about what it means to be a good citizen." In response to the survey question on civic responsibilities, one school mentioned their application of SCANS skills and another wrote that social responsibility was part of their schoolwide outcomes for students.

Students are involved in curricular planning. The model's Principle 5 reads, "The governing practical metaphor of the school should be student-as-worker rather than the more familiar metaphor of teacher-as-deliverer-of-instructional-services. Accordingly, a prominent pedagogy will be coaching and guiding to enable students to understand how they learn and thus to teach themselves and each other."

Teachers are encouraged to use varied learning materials and teaching strategies. Students are provided with many resources and perspectives so that they may make their own decisions. Teachers are learning coaches and may use a textbook as one source of information, but not as the sole source for a particular topic. Teachers

are empowered to develop interesting and valuable activities, projects, and lessons. Schools surveyed listed many teaching strategies such as Socratic seminars, exhibitions, "Week Without Walls" program, leadership retreats, and portfolios.

Interdisciplinary team teaching is used to develop connections between core subject areas and real-life situations. It is believed that forming these connections leads to a more interesting and rewarding educational experience for students. Students are coached as active learners and empowered to take responsibility, along with their teachers and parents, for their own education. Students may serve on local or state advisory councils and work with people in the community. Reflection is viewed by the model as an integral part of students' educational development and character. The Coalition's process encourages reflection both before and after an experience or event.

Sources:
Coalition of Essential Schools, Home Page www.essentialschools.org/aboutus/phil/whole_sch/whole_sch.html.

Cushman, K. (1999). Essential school structure and design: Boldest moves get the best results. *Horace*, *15* (5). Retrieved 2002, from http://www.essentialschools.org/pubs/horace/15/v15n05.html.

MacMullen, M. M. (1996). *Taking stock of a school reform effort*. Occasional Paper Series, No. 2. Providence, RI: Annenberg Institute for School Reform, Brown University.

Northwest Regional Educational Laboratory (2001). *The catalog of school reform models*. Retrieved 2002, from http://www.nwrel.org/scpd/catalog/index.shtml.

Sizer, T. (1997). *Horace's compromise: The dilemma of the American high school,* 3rd edition. Boston, MA: Mariner Books/Houghton Mifflin Company.

Sizer, T. R. & Smith, H. (1997). *Horace's hope: What works for the American high school*. Boston, MA: Mariner Books/Houghton Mifflin Company.

COMMUNITY FOR LEARNING

1301 Cecil B. Moore Avenue, Philadelphia, PA 19122-6091, 800-892-5550, 215-204-5130 fax
http://www.temple.edu/LSS

Score: Compatible

"Community for Learning is a system of management that allows you to meet the needs of all levels of students." – *Sue Goold, educator, Willow Hill School District, Pennsylvania*

Features:

♦ Model creates collaborative relationships among the school, home, libraries, museums, and other places where students can learn.

♦ Health and human services component.

♦ Site-specific implementation design.

♦ Professional Development and teaming.

♦ Adaptive Learning Environments instruction.

♦ Instructional strategies and support.

Background: Community for Learning (CFL), formerly known as the Adaptive Learning Environments Model, was developed by Margaret C. Wang, Executive Director of the Temple University Center for Research in Human Development and Education in 1990. CFL was influenced by more than three decades of research and practical experience that show implementing innovative school programs results in higher student achievement.

Premise: The model is based on research that shows that student learning is affected by multiple learning environments in addition to school, including home, workplace, community organizations, social service agencies, higher learning institutions, church, and others who make up a "community for learning." Students can achieve academic success when schools are linked with community institutions. Parent/community engagement is paramount.

Design: CFL focuses on improving student learning in all subject areas using a comprehensive improvement framework. It does this by introducing broad goals to change the conventional management and organization of the school, for example, using flexible scheduling and small learning communities that work together to create interdisciplinary curricula and bringing parents, educators, students, and community members together to define a coherent vision of the school.

The model provides data on program implementation and student performance for staff to use in devising action plans to meet classroom and school-level goals. According to the model developer, these data-based improvement plans are revised on an ongoing basis based on student progress. CFL coordinates practices and policies that have been used in classrooms and reconfigures those ideas to create a coherent program that has a positive effect on student achievement. The program consists of three main elements: *Schoolwide Restructuring*, *Adaptive Instructional Strategies and Practices*, and *Family and Community Support*. The model is emphatic in its communication to schools that its design does not "thrust a different curriculum upon the school, require hiring many new staff members, or throw out everything old in favor of something new."

The *Schoolwide Restructuring* effort includes developing a school plan based on resources available in the school and staff expertise. Professional development and teaming provides support for schools to engage in a team approach to raising students' academic achievement. Teams of regular teachers, specialists, and administrators are formed to address the individual needs of diverse students. A database for professional development provides an ongoing, individually tailored program.

Adaptive Instructional Strategies and Practices uses an inclusive approach designed to meet the learning needs of a diverse group of students. Tasks involved include a prescriptive process for institutional planning and monitoring of the school's progress, developing individualized learning plans, and charting student advancement. The instructional process focuses on getting students to achieve high academic standards, including adopting a student-centered instructional process that incorporates subject-matter learning. The model encourages interactive teaching that provides "on-the-spot" educating, adjusting and reassessing student needs regularly, and reviewing lessons for small groups of students who need extra assistance. A classroom management strategy is developed to support student success. This requires fostering students' individual responsibility and establishing and communicating rules and procedures, as well as coordinating with support services and personnel resources. According to the model, the classroom design should provide an environment that supports effective learning. Arranging classroom space to encourage student movement and organizing materials in a systemic manner for easy access and use is encouraged to foster student independence and individual responsibility.

Family and Community Support is part of the model design that links families and community to student learning, emphasizing shared responsibility and the use of existing resources. The model works with the school to develop a systematic plan that strengthens communication among the school, families, and the community. Connections are made with health and human services programs as part of a comprehensive system of service delivery that supports students' healthy development and academic success. Links are made with local libraries, museums, and other community assets to create extended learning environments and enhance student achievement.

Evidence of Results: In the American Institutes for Research's *An Educator's Guide to Schoolwide Reform,* Community for Learning is rated as having "Promising evidence of positive effects on student achievement." This promising rating indicates that three or more studies, using rigorous methodologies, show positive effects of the model's approach to student achievement.

CFL lists progress toward student success in three of its demonstration sites. In a middle school in Pennsylvania where 93 percent of students live in poverty, 78 percent are Latino, there is a 38 percent student turnover rate, and 38 percent of teachers have less than three years of teaching experience, the model was able to reduce the school's dropout rate, eliminate the dropout rate among special education students, and get 48 percent of 11th grade students to perform at grade level.

In an elementary school in Houston, Texas where 89 percent of students qualify for free or reduced lunch, 74 percent are Latino, nearly half of students require bilingual education or ESL instruction, 58 percent of students enter or leave in the middle of the school year, and there is a 28 percent teacher turnover rate, the model was able to raise the level of the school to become a "recognized" school in the district where 90 percent of students met the minimum expectations in reading and 78 percent in math, student perceptions and attitudes about the school were improved, and the school received approval to operate as a public charter school.

In an elementary school in Washington, DC, where 94 percent of students are eligible for free or reduced lunch, implementation of the model raised the school's rank in the district from 119 among 121 elementary schools in reading, to 46th, and 120th in math to 24th.

Compatibility with Service-Learning: It is surprising that the model rated itself as being *compatible* and not highly compatible since one-third of its design hinges on a goal called Family and Community Support. The design does not share detailed examples of what it means by a plan to strengthen communication with the community, or to link with community assets such as a museum or university, but there is room to interpret ways for service-learning to fit smoothly within the model's design. The model's adaptive learning practice that includes student-centered instruction and "cross-discipline teaming" is highly compatible with the ideals of service-learning. If the instruction is meant to be truly student-centered and based upon ways to encourage students to take responsibility for their own learning, service-learning would fit since it has proven to be a powerful motivator for engaging students in learning.

Sources:
Community for Learning, Information Packet (2001). Home Page http://www.temple.edu/LSS/cfl_prgovr.htm.

Herman, R. (1999). *An educator's guide to schoolwide reform*. Retrieved 2002, from http://www.aasa.org/issues_and_insights/district_organization/Reform/index.htm.

Northwest Regional Educational Laboratory (2001). *The catalog of school reform models*. Retrieved 2002, from http://www.nwrel.org/scpd/catalog/index.shtml.

Wang, M. C., Haertel, G. D., & Walberg, H. J. (1997). *What do we know: Widely implemented school improvement programs. A special report issued by the Laboratory for Student Success*. Philadelphia, PA: Center for Research in Human Development, Temple University.

COMMUNITY LEARNING CENTERS

c/o Designs for Learning,1021 Bandana Boulevard E. Suite 214,St. Paul, MN 55108
651-645-0200, 651-645-0240 fax
http://www.designlearn.net

Score: Compatible

"A learner-centered approach personalizes education and makes it relevant to students' lives. The end result is far greater achievement at conventional academics and real-life competencies of a productive worker, responsible citizen, and lifelong learner." – *Designs for Learning Staff*

Features:

♦ Brain-based, child-centered, applied and experiential learning.

♦ Educators provide students with opportunities to have experiences that elicit strong positive emotions about learning.

♦ School campus includes the world outside the classroom.

Background: Designs for Learning is the developer of the Community Learning Centers (CLC) and continues to revise and enhance the CLC design. The design began in 1992 with a grant from New American Schools and originated from the work of thirty researchers who looked at educational research and best practices intensively for over one year. The results of their findings made up the original CLC document. Their design concept was field tested in nine sites (urban, rural, Indian reservation, and charter schools) in Minnesota.

Premise: All learners enjoy school every day and are becoming highly effective and responsible citizens. Every student has five major life transformational outcomes. These include productive worker, responsible citizen, problem solver, self-directed lifelong learner, and creative, healthy individual.

Design: The Community Learning Centers program is a broad comprehensive school design that aims to dramatically increase the achievement of all learners, Pre-K-adult. The model provides guidance to schools and districts in the following areas: systemic change, negotiated change, outcomes and assessments, program and curriculum, process of learning, personal learning plan and advisory program, allocation of resources, staffing, staff development, technology utilization, students as resources, management, parent involvement, partnerships and social services, program choice, lifelong learning, facility and learning environment, and sustaining change.

CLC uses an educational approach called brain-based learning. Brain-based learning is described by the developer as a systemic approach based on the work of many scholars and practitioners that "… encompasses many practices known to advance permanent learning." Brain-based learning provides for rapid, deep, and satisfying learning. Brain compatible education focuses on four basic building blocks of the brain's learning: patterns of understanding, programs for action, feedback, and safety and security. The model acknowledges brain-based learning as a constructivist approach that is epitomized in experiential learning and community service projects. Based on the brain-based learning theory, the process of learning, in order to register permanently in the student's brain, must be meaningful to the student, applied within 24 hours, and have an emotional impact.

The school acts as the broker in arranging learning experiences in the community for real world application. Community Learning Centers emphasize active learning environments such as media centers, production studios, discovery centers, theaters of learning, labs, community-based learning, and workstations for various computer applications. Each student, or learner, has a personal learning plan for recording goals, experiences to reach goals, and progress toward goals, as well as an advisor who meets periodically with them and their parents to review the plan.

The model's curriculum is based on achievement of standards and outcomes through powerful learning experiences and is defined as all the experiences of the learner irrespective of place, time, or person. These outcomes come with a list of sample learning activities. Under one heading called "responsible citizen," for example, curriculum activities are as follows.

- Complete a volunteer responsibility with a community organization.

- Write a cogent letter to the editorial page on a significant issue.

- Participate in a mock trial.

- Serve in an elementary school, helping teachers with students.

- Learn parliamentary procedure and how to conduct meetings.

Students plan projects with the help of their teachers. They also do this in groups and with a personal learning plan tailored to their needs. The model suggests that a computer program or database be created to manage the record keeping that this type of project-learning can generate. The database is used to list the activities done to reach outcomes. Questions in the database may include what and how the student will do the activity, where the student will do the activity, the degree of subject matter content present, the degree of achievement in each academic area, the status of the activity, notes from the teacher, and so on. Every student is different so, for example, in the case of a student with weak writing skills, the advisor would adjust the student's personal learning plan to include an activity or learning system that would assist them in this area. Instruction is provided in the context of need, and according to

the developer, "As students accumulate hundreds of project experiences, their knowledge and skill base grows rapidly and feeds upon itself in cumulative fashion." Flexible use of time is encouraged, including longer blocks of time to focus on student-driven projects. How this is implemented varies from school to school.

CLC provides a rubric to help the school, district, community, parents, or school board assess progress on the Community Learning Centers' Benchmarks and Indicators. A rubric for one benchmark is:

CLC Key Feature	Phase I Beginning/ Good	Phase II Implementing/ Better	Phase III Realizing/ Best
Students are resources for the program	*Students as resources.* Students' input is sought in development of projects.	Students' ideas and participation are consistently incorporated into the development and assessment of the learning program.	Students are treated as resources that, as part of their studies, contribute to the program and community, and are challenged and supported to become lifelong, self-directed learners.
	Personal Learning Plans(PLP). Students participate in developing a PLP, with input from the advisor and parent(s).	PLPs are in place for all students and define individual goals; most planning and documentation of learning experiences to meet the goals is connected to the PLP.	Each student's PLP serves the functions of: establishing individual goals; planning learning experiences to reach goals; and documenting progress toward attainment of goals. Students undertake responsibility for developing the PLP.

CLC Key Feature	Phase I Beginning/ Good	Phase II Implementing/ Better	Phase III Realizing/ Best
Students are resources for the program	*Students are stakeholders in maintaining technology-enriched environments.* Some student projects or specific classes use computers and other technology tools.	Students often use technology to enhance learning and multiply productivity.	Students routinely use technology to enhance learning and multiply productivity. Some students help empower others in the use of technology.

Because the model believes that most students are "ill prepared for work or future learning" and "do not have a salable skill upon graduation," it has recommended that the SCANS skills that came out of a report by the U.S. Department of Labor serve as a guide for curriculum as "students and staff together determine content and methods of learning."

Evidence of Results: No current external evaluation was found.

Compatibility with Service-Learning: The model scored itself as *compatible* with service-learning. Yet, many of the model's design elements are highly compatible with service-learning, including the following list.

- Students are treated as resources that, as part of their studies, contribute to the program and community and are challenged and supported to become self-directed, lifelong learners.

- Curricula include opportunities to serve others and solve real problems.

- CLC uses the community as the school campus and focus for curriculum. The school acts as a broker in arranging learning experiences within and beyond its walls for real-world application.

- CLC emphasizes learning rather than teaching. The role of the teacher as a facilitator and orchestrator of learning.

- CLC helps schools garner the support of a variety of community groups, including governmental bodies, school administration, local businesses, agencies, parents, and other community members.

- CLC strives to integrate and facilitate access to social services, preferably at the school site.

The foundation of the CLC model rests on the belief that learning must be applicable to the "real world," relevant to life beyond school. According to the model, project-based learning builds on students' ideas and interest, and should be happening in all CLC schools. The model directs schools to draw on community resources – organizations, businesses, local government and social services as well as individuals – while creating curricula, designing projects, and serving community needs through service-learning projects. "In practice," says the model, "this element has been difficult to implement, and in some cases has been implemented with varying degrees of success." Still, CLC, asserts, its schools would have more connection to the local community than a typical public school.

Each student has considerable input on their learning experience through their personal learning plan (PLP) which is based on the student's interests, needs and goals. Learning activities flow from the plan. "We seek to follow the 'world as classroom' philosophy, with teachers encouraged to use a wide variety of media in addition to or instead of textbooks. Ideally, students seek out their own resources for projects, whether print, electronic, or human," wrote the developer.

Concepts of brain-based learning that greatly support experiential learning are central to the CLC model. CLC schools typically use interdisciplinary strategies, often using multi-age classrooms as well. Portfolios are in use at CLC schools; and at the middle and secondary level, student presentations are typically expected at the end of major units. "We recognize the importance of reflection and need to do more to build it into the CLC programs," wrote the developer.

Alternative assessments are a critical part of the model and need to become more rigorous to generate objective data that can be reported. Currently, most schools using the model are charter schools.

Sources:
Community Learning Centers model by Designs for Learning (2002) Home Page http://www.designlearn.net.

Community Learning Centers Design Specifications (1999, June). St. Paul, MN: Designs for Learning.

Jennings, W. (1996). *Joining hands: A resource book on integrating experiential learning into the school curriculum.* St. Paul, MN: Designs for Learning.

Jennings, W., Adelmann, A. J., Smith, N. (2000). *Charter schools: Creating and sustaining family-friendly schools*. St. Paul, MN: Designs for Learning. Retrieved 2002, from http://www.uscharterschools.org/gb/familyfriendly/.

Shaping Educational Initiatives. Designs for Learning Information Packet (2001).

CO-NECT SCHOOLS

1770 Massachusetts Ave #301, Cambridge, MA 02140, 617-995-3156, 617-995-3103 fax
http://www.co-nect.com

Score: Highly Compatible

"We focus not only on the fundamentals, such as literacy and core math skills, but also on applying academic content to real-world problems that require critical thinking skills." – *Co-nect Schools*

Features:

♦ Provides methods, tools, training, and technical assistance to help schools prepare students for a "lifetime of learning, productive work, and responsible citizenship–in ways that are consistent with each individual's special strengths, interests, and aspirations."

♦ Emphasizes the use of projects and other purposeful activities and interactions that result in deep understanding of subject matter, higher-order thinking, application of academic knowledge to real problems, and authentic, high-quality work.

♦ Onsite school consultants help schools align curriculum, assessment, and instruction, and provide professional development in areas of need.

Background: Co-nect was founded in 1992 by the Educational Technologies Group at BBN Corporation (Bolt, Beranek and Newman, a research and development firm based in Cambridge, Massachusetts) in response to a call for proposals from a newly-formed Washington, D.C.-based nonprofit group of corporate chief executives, the New American Schools Development Corporation (now New American Schools NAS) NAS' mission is to create school designs that help local communities create their own replicable "break-the-mold" schools, thereby dramatically improving educational achievement for a majority of students in all schools.

Premise: Young people learn best in schools that emphasize thoughtful discourse, authentic work, and the investigation of rigorous academic subject matter in the context of problems and issues that have meaning beyond the classroom.

Design: Co-nect's school model is based on an integrated set of research-based strategies for improving student achievement. The strategies are supported by a body of research on the features of high-performing schools. These include educators' shared (cross-grade, cross-subject) responsibility for student achievement in reading, writing, mathematics, and other core subject areas; emphasis on practical application of knowledge to real-world tasks as a way of building understanding and engagement; regular diagnostic assessments; and the use of technology to support higher-order thinking, especially in mathematics and science.

Students in Co-nect schools engage in a variety of community-oriented activities. For example, at ALL School in Worcester, Massachusetts, the first Co-nect school in the country, students in the upper school (grades 9-12) are required to take part in community internship programs involving more than 100 community organizations. As part of the "Kids 'n Blues" project in Memphis, Tennessee (funded by the Bell South Corporation) students wrote lyrics for songs, performed them, and created and marketed their own CD. Elementary and middle school students in South Florida studied violence in schools, then produced original videos as part of the "End the Violence" project. (The students plan to petition the School Board to make the video available to all Broward County Schools.) Florida high schools have shown leadership in an organ and tissue transplant project called Life 101. Two Miami-Dade County Schools are partnering with the South Florida Blood Bank to assist with blood donations. As part of this project, students developed an informational website in English and Spanish and a marketing campaign to target young, Hispanic, first-time blood donors. Students developed community projects that were submitted to Co-nect's annual student project from one of these Florida high schools.

Through the Co-nect model, students learn how to work together as a team and understand and respect the importance of revision and reflection as they strive to achieve high standards. Students are encouraged to produce final products, work that meets marketplace specifications. With this in mind, students quickly understand the value of collaboration, deadlines, and an aptitude for doing whatever it takes to do high quality work.

Co-nect staff help teachers critically examine the school's curriculum as well as their own instructional techniques. Co-nect staff provide classroom-based professional development activities to help teachers deepen their content knowledge and apply research on best practices. The model also encourages a team-based approach to improving student achievement in the school.

Other key features of the model are:

- A school-based School Design Team (instructional leadership team) assumes responsibility for managing the change process within the school. The team is led by the building principal, and includes a Co-nect school facilitator, teachers, parents, and influential community members.

- Action Teams use materials provided by Co-nect to research issues, develop, and recommend a concrete plan of action.

- The model encourages the formation of Clusters, small learning communities in which teachers stay with the same group of students for two years or more.

- As part of the Co-nect Critical Friends program, teachers participate in structured site visits to other schools in the network and prepare confidential reports.

- School Consultants provide onsite support for a cluster of schools in a district or region, visiting each school approximately twice a month to conduct workshops, and working directly with teachers in the classroom.

- Participating schools are required to appoint a School Facilitator, an educator who facilitates implementation of the Co-nect model in his or her own school.

Co-nect works with teachers and administration to help them incorporate:

- Benchmarking as a means of setting goals and measuring progress. The Co-nect model is based on benchmarks derived from features of high-performing schools.

- Portfolio Assessment and Audit that uses student work as an indicator of achievement is used as one of several measures of student and school progress. The audit of student achievement, based on samples of student work, is used alongside test data as a longitudinal measure of schoolwide student achievement.

- Curriculum Mapping as a process to develop a shared understanding of what is being taught, to whom, and when. Curriculum mapping helps remove duplication of efforts, identifies missing pieces, and highlights areas for potential collaboration or integration across subject areas or grade levels.

Professional Development and training in the Co-nect system includes: Facilitator's Institute, Foundation Workshop, Mini-Sabbatical, National Conference, Co-nect Exchange, and Principals' Summit. Other tools and methods in the model's design include:

- Project-Based Teaching and Learning: an educational approach that emphasizes learning of essential knowledge and critical skills through work on authentic issues and problems.

- Project Builder: an online tool that Co-nect teachers can use to plan standards-based curriculum projects.

- Rubrics: a formal set of guidelines for measuring the quality of student work. Schools are encouraged to use a set of rubrics to compare their own professional practices against the Co-nect Benchmarks.

- School Progress Review: a review of a school's progress in respect to the Co-nect Benchmarks.

- School Project Fair: a public event at which community members have an opportunity to view and discuss student project work.

- Solid Start™: an introductory customized professional development plan and action plan for implementation of the model.

- The Exchange: an online resource for Co-nect schools, offering "telecollaborative" projects, curriculum resources, discussion areas, training modules, and community-building utilities.

Evidence of Results: A national study from researchers at Boston College compared achievement gains in 24 Co-nect schools that had recently adopted the Co-Nect model with gains in similar schools in the same districts. The study revealed that most schools improved student achievement and four had outpaced gains in comparison schools.

An independent study conducted and released by Cincinnati Public Schools showed that Co-nect schools "exceeded district wide average changes and the average improvements made in district magnet schools during the same period."

Another independent study conducted at the University of Memphis and University of Tennessee-Knoxville from 1996-1998 found that four Co-nect schools in Memphis had shown stronger achievement gains across all subject areas over two years on Tennessee's Value-Added Assessment System.

Compatibility with Service-Learning: The model scored itself as *highly compatible* with service-learning. One of the backbones of the design places an emphasis on project-based learning where authentic projects are combined with portfolios and performance-based assessments. Co-nect schools involved in the survey agreed; "All projects have real-life driving questions guiding focus towards mastery of standards," and "One of the benchmarks is project building. This is where students apply standards-based knowledge."

Community partnerships are "strongly encouraged" by the model. A Co-nect school wrote, "Projects may include learning about natural disasters common to an area. The model includes a reading program designed to meet the needs of all students. The community is strongly encouraged to form partnerships with the school." Another school revealed that the model meets directly with the community and does some benchmark training with parents. Southwest Miami High School has a track record for development and implementation of original student-developed projects that tackle a community-based problem or challenge. One project, Reading Bees, features an after school literacy experience and reading nights at the local library with high school students reading to their younger peers and Co-nect staff working with parents on the ways they can help their children become stronger readers. Another Co-nect school involved students in designing and building a home for a disadvantaged family in their school community. Co-nect schools partner with organizations like the American Red Cross which have strong partnerships in their community.

The model strongly encourages schools to focus on educating the whole child and that means "preparing all students for a lifetime of learning, productive work, and responsible citizenship." A Co-nect school wrote, "Many projects address civics and government standards as directed in social studies, such as one for the Red Cross."

Co-nect encourages students to play an active role in their own learning. According to one Co-nect school, students may choose to develop their own projects around local needs or interests as long as the project is driven by standards.

Teaching and instructional strategies that support service-learning are used by the Co-nect model: project-based learning, cooperative learning, self-assessment, and rubric evaluations. Interdisciplinary teaching is encouraged. "Teachers may choose to work as teams horizontally and vertically," wrote one school.

The design supports student reflection and says, "Thoughtful classroom discourse [is] strongly encouraged." "Comprehensive assessment is one of the five benchmarks of the model," said one school, and "Rubrics, portfolios, presentations, models, and demonstrations are all encouraged and are a major component of assessment," said another.

Sources:
Cincinnati Public Schools (1999). *New American Schools designs: An analysis of program results in District schools*. Cincinnati, OH.

Quesada, A. (2000). What works: Projects, portfolios, and performance-based assessments. *Technology and Learning*, *20* (12). Pull-out flyer made for Co-nect.

Ross, S. M., Sanders, W. L., Stringfield, S., Wang, L.W., & Wright, S. (1999). *Two-and three-year achievement results on the Tennessee value-added assessment system for restructuring schools in Memphis.* Memphis, TN: Center for Research in Education Policy, University of Memphis.

Russell, M., & Robinson, R. (2000). *Co-nect retrospective outcomes study.* Boston, MA: Center for the Study of Testing, Evaluation and Educational Policy, Boston College.

Wittman, S. (2000, January). New national program connects kids and technology. Hometown highlights: News from South Florida. *South Florida Parenting*, p. 18.

CORE KNOWLEDGE

801 East High Street, Charlottesville, VA 22902, 804-977-7550, 804-977-0021 fax
http://www.coreknowledge.org

Score: Compatible

"The Core Knowledge Sequence represents the first major effort to specify a common core curriculum for children in American schools. Unlike other countries, including France, Japan, Korea, Sweden, and Denmark, where the use of a common core curriculum is often regarded as having led to more nearly universal competence and excellence, the United States does not have a national common core curriculum" – *E. D. Hirsch, Jr.*

Features:

♦ Back-to-basics, Pre-K-8 sequential curriculum that builds on core subjects grade-by-grade, leaving the rest of the curriculum planning to the school.

♦ Specifies content, not process.

Background: Core Knowledge was developed by the Core Knowledge Foundation, an independent, nonprofit, nonpartisan organization founded by E. D. Hirsch, Jr., education author and professor at the University of Virginia. The Foundation conducts research on curricula, offers workshops for teachers, and serves as the network hub for Core Knowledge schools.

Premise: Students learn more effectively when instruction follows the "basic psychological principle that we learn new knowledge by building on what we already know."

Design: The key feature of the design is the *Core Knowledge Sequence* that builds on knowledge from previous grades, providing a solid foundation of the basic subjects taught in school. "For example, in fifth grade World History, study of the Renaissance builds on earlier studies of ancient Greece (second grade), ancient Rome (third grade), and the Middle Ages (fourth grade). Or, in science, the basic concept of the atom, introduced in first grade, leads by fifth grade to an understanding of how atomic properties are organized in the Periodic Table." The model encourages schools to align the *Core Knowledge Sequence* with their state standards.

Schools appoint a school-based Core Knowledge coordinator who will work with the principal to help support implementation. Teachers must be provided 90 minutes of common planning time per week. "Common planning time is essential to the success of Core Knowledge implementation." A sequential reading and math program of proven effectiveness must be chosen by the school among a list of effective programs approved by the model.

The model's curriculum design is highly prescriptive and teachers are expected to teach all of the topics in the *Core Knowledge Sequence* at the grade levels specified. The model asks for 80 percent faculty buy-in and requires the school to obtain support from their district, placing the district representative in a responsible position for assisting with implementation and evaluation of Core Knowledge and answering district-level questions that arise during the first three years of implementation.

Year One includes a school orientation to the model and a leadership institute where school staff are formally introduced to the theory and research behind the development of the *Core Knowledge Sequence*. With a Core Knowledge coordinator, a school will discuss strategies that can be used in developing the implementation plan and the role of the school leadership team.

In Years Two and Three, the model provides advanced professional development training for new teacher training and submits progress reports on the schoolwide implementation. School staff are engaged in discussing strategies for sustained implementation. Teachers are asked to apply the elements learned in Year One as they write units of study, select appropriate resources, develop meaningful instructional procedures and activities, and utilize effective methods of assessment.

The model has created workshop materials such as a Teacher's Kit and a School Start-up Kit. The kits include lesson plans, CDs, videos, publications, and other tools for "ramping up" implementation of the design. The model also points schools to other resources such as maps, globes and other teacher reference books for the classroom.

The model asks that the school's implementation plan address finding resources, creating common planning time, communicating with and involving parents and community members, integrating technology, involving administrators and teacher specialists, and addressing other areas of need, as determined by the school. Schools are asked to develop an evaluation plan to determine progress, identify strengths and weaknesses of their implementation plan, and measure student success. They are also directed to administer the Core Knowledge curriculum-referenced tests in grades one through five at the end of each year. Reading and mathematics assessments are included with selected programs chosen by the school.

The model believes that its design benefits students, educators, parents, and the community in a number of ways. For students, it provides a broad base of knowledge and a rich vocabulary, motivating them to learn. For the school, the design provides an academic focus and encourages consistency in instruction, provides a plan for coherent, sequenced learning from grade to grade, promotes a community of learners—adults and children, and becomes an effective tool for lesson planning and communication among teachers. For parents and the community, it provides a clear outline of what children are expected to learn in school, encourages parents to participate in their children's education, both at home and in school, and provides opportunities for community members to help obtain and provide instructional resources.

Evidence of Results: In the American Institutes for Research's *An Educator's Guide to Schoolwide Reform*, the model was rated as having "Promising evidence of positive effects on student achievement. This promising rating indicates that three or more studies, using rigorous methodologies, show positive effects of the model's approach on student achievement."

In 1997, researchers from Johns Hopkins University looked at 12 Core Knowledge schools located in seven states, situated in various communities (urban, rural, suburban), racial, and socioeconomic contexts. Of the 12, six schools were listed by the Core Knowledge Foundation as relatively advanced in their implementation of the model's curriculum and six schools were deemed as promising implementation sites. The study followed the 1995-1996 first and third-grade cohort at all schools, including a set of control schools.

Researchers were able to find qualitative evidence that showed the model increased self-confidence in students. "Educators at almost all of the schools recounted stories of their students approaching visitors to the school to tell them about what they had recently learned." A teacher at one school commented: "They think they're big people, important people, because they're talking about the seven continents and Ancient Egypt." The study also revealed that teachers felt the spiraling curriculum in the design helped students retain more information from year to year. "I am hearing teachers in the grades ahead say that they don't have to back up as far as they used to," said one teacher. Core Knowledge appeared to lessen the need for reteaching concepts at the beginning of the school year. Also, teachers credited the work that goes into preparing to teach Core Knowledge as one of the things that makes their work more rewarding. A teacher explained: "The energy I put into it makes it more meaningful for me."

The Hopkins study stated that Core Knowledge is good for all students, citing educators' claims at many of the schools that one of the major benefits of the curriculum is that it can meet the needs of all students. "It's like a gifted curriculum for all kids," said one principal. Another teacher stated, "I think the strength of the Core Knowledge program is that the students, no matter what their ability level, can pick up that background information. And that's the idea of leveling the playing field."

Compatibility with Service-Learning: The model scored itself as *compatible* with service-learning, and can provide curricular support to a school that has chosen to implement service-learning. Each school has the authority to use their time for teaching Core Knowledge as it best suits them.

Core Knowledge allows the classroom teacher flexibility in teaching methods and instruction. Teachers are encouraged to write curriculum and teach Core Knowledge as creatively as they choose. Teachers and students may plan curricular activities together if they wish. Core Knowledge is not text book driven. "Core Knowledge is about content. Instructional methods are left up to the discretion of the teacher," wrote the developer. The model encourages connections from content area to content area, and, according to the model, many Core Knowledge schools opt to team teach. Students make connections from their everyday learning to real-life situations in conversations, in museums, on television, and in their reading. Teachers are encouraged to use assessments beyond tests and quizzes. Core Knowledge classrooms vary from school to school, and time for student reflection may be incorporated into classroom activities.

Sources:
Core Knowledge Foundation, Home Page http://www.coreknowledge.org/.

Herman, R. (Project Director) (1999). *An educator's guide to schoolwide reform*. Retrieved 2002, from http://www.aasa.org/issues_and_insights/district_organization/Reform/index.htm.

Northwest Regional Educational Laboratory (2001). *The catalog of school reform models*. Retrieved 2002, from http://www.nwrel.org/scpd/catalog/index.shtml.

Stringfield, S., Datnow, A., & Nunnery, J. (1997). *First year evaluation of the implementation of the Core Knowledge sequence: Qualitative Report*. Baltimore, MD: The Johns Hopkins University.

Different Ways of Knowing

5670 Wilshire Blvd. 20th Floor, Los Angeles, CA 90036-5623, 323-525-0042, 323-525-0408 fax
http://www.dwoknet.galef.org

Score: Highly Compatible

"Start with the natural wonder of children, support them with your knowledge of how we learn, and reveal to them your own passion for learning." – *Linda Johannesen, president, The Galef Institute*

Features:

♦ Philosophy, curriculum module and professional development for grades K-8 in standards-driven student-centered learning.

♦ Curriculum integrates the study of history and social studies with literature and writing; math and science; and the performing, visual and media arts.

♦ Inquiry-based, arts-infused, interdisciplinary, professional development initiative.

Background: Different Ways of Knowing (DWoK) was created by Galef Institute in Los Angeles, California. Galef Institute, founded in 1989 by Andrew G. Galef, is a nonprofit educational organization whose primary goal is comprehensive school reform. Andrew G. Galef served on the California State Commission for the Establishment of Academic Content and Performance Standards. He is Chairman Emeritus of the Board of Advisors to the Entrepreneurial Studies Center of UCLA's John Anderson Graduate School of Management.

Premise: As teachers and students experience DWoK, they will be able to create a content-rich classroom learning community. The change in both teachers and students will begin to change the school and "influence the learning life of their school." All stakeholders involved will become colleagues in the transformation of the school into an exciting place for all children and adults to learn.

Design: DWoK provides a framework for hands-on, student-centered, standards-based learning that guides classroom teaching, and continuous professional development for educators. It uses themes to develop the multiple intelligences of children (based on author Howard Gardner's 1983 seminal work, *Frames of Mind: The Theory of Multiple Intelligences*), making the academic curriculum more meaningful and accessible to all students. The model is based on the seven intelligences in Gardner's book:

1. Linguistic—sensitive to sounds and rhythms;

2. Musical—sensitive to rhythm, pitch, and timbre;

3. Logical-mathematical—easily discern patterns and relationship;

4. Spatial—sensitive to images and forms;

5. Bodily-kinesthetic—aware of mind-body coordination;

6. Interpersonal—sensitive to moods, temperament, and relationships; and

7. Intrapersonal—possess self-knowledge and insight.

DWoK provides a variety of theme-based learning resources from publishers, including childrens' literature, reference materials, transparencies, audio and videotapes, and computer software. The model helps teachers and students "expand their literacy spectrum to include all human intelligences and aptitudes." Schools are assisted in adapting instruction outside of traditional sources to include a variety of tools, including visual, performing, and media arts.

A classroom community is built that encourages shared responsibility for classroom management and learning, and promotes an understanding of democratic ideals. The model provides guidelines and resources to assess student learning and provides a common language for teachers and their colleagues to create a meaningful educational partnership among the school, parents, and community.

Each curriculum module features an extensive Teacher Planning Guide, including standards-driven content, instructional strategies, and planning resources. The modules are integrated around real problems, have themes, topics and guiding questions, and are linked to curriculum standards in history, social studies, science, mathematics, and the literary, visual, performing, and media arts. The curriculum modules capitalize on students' curiosity, personal experience, and a desire to solve real problems, and pursue ideas that are of value to them.

Professional development for teachers, administrators, specialists, families, and community members is provided in summer institutes and full-day workshops held throughout the year. Participating sites are matched with an interdisciplinary support team of coaches, including teachers experienced in the DWoK design. There is monthly on-site coaching, an interactive website and an annual two-day leadership institute for principals and lead teachers.

Students are allowed to become partners in the educational process. They build a repertoire of knowledge and skills needed for life through the model's curriculum modules that are built on connections of one learning event to another. According to the model developer, successful participation for all children should include the arts so that intuition is balanced with cognition. Learning events are designed "to encourage children to use their minds well, to think creatively, and to solve problems in different ways." Through the arts, the model's philosophy holds, children and teachers continually expand the ways in which they think, perceive, and interpret. Students receive instruction on interacting with others and gain confidence as problem solvers.

Evidence of Results: The American Institutes for Research's *An Educator's Guide to Schoolwide Reform*, rates the model as having "Promising evidence of positive effects on student achievement. This promising rating indicates that three or more studies, using rigorous methodologies, show positive effects of the model's approach on student achievement."

Two major research projects looked at the model's influence on standardized test scores, state assessment results, student writing samples, surveys from students and teachers and classroom observations. A UCLA-led longitudinal study of 1,000 children in four school districts in Los Angeles and Boston over three years between 1991 and 1994, found a positive correlation between students' test scores and their number of years with the DWoK model. Gains of eight percentile points on standardized tests were seen in vocabulary, comprehension, and other measures of language arts, and higher student scores were seen on written tests of social studies content knowledge. Researchers noted that higher grades "by one-half grade point increased cognitive engagement and intrinsic interest in the humanities increased levels of achievement and motivation over time, as opposed to patterns of eroding motivation for non-Different Ways of Knowing students."

The second study was led by the University of Louisville and the University of Kentucky, and compared the implementation of 24 DWoK schools in Kentucky to non-DWoK schools from 1993 to 1995. Researchers found: the KIRIS statewide assessment of 4th grade students showed seven percent greater gains in reading arts and humanities compared to schools statewide; 10 percent greater gains in social studies; 25 percent greater gains in math scores; and seven percent greater gains in science. Researchers noted involvement of the model's students in their classroom activities and greater interest in their schoolwork.

Compatibility with Service-Learning: The model scored itself as *highly compatible* with service-learning. Through the model design, teachers discover multiple ways to make curriculum connections throughout the school day, giving children opportunities to learn content through interdisciplinary connections that encourage flexible use of time and scheduling. The design "celebrates and builds on the strengths of students as creative, capable learners." The model also provides guidance for educators to help students apply their knowledge and skills to real-life situations. According to the model, DWoK helps students understand and develop an appreciation for their community. "Students explore resources outside of their classrooms and invite outside experts in to share information. As reflective learners, DWoK students connect what they've learned to their own lives–this is an integral part of the design of DWoK curriculum tools." One school that participated in the survey reported, "The Communities unit in 3rd grade teaches how to keep the environment clean, whether it be home, forest, ocean, or river."

Developing civic skills and competencies "is a strong DWoK component." The model's curriculum opens doors for students to make civic connections to their own community and to find that they have the power to change the way other people see and think about civic issues and challenges, i.e., ecological problems and governing issues. One school described "What's Up in the Neighborhood" as being a significant part of the program. Students explore, refine, choose, and elaborate meaning over multiple drafts of their work and choose to "express evolving understanding through a variety of presentational formats." Teachers create group and individual projects that define meaningful ways to relate to curriculum content.

According to the model, "teachers use the DWoK curriculum as a tool to launch compelling ways to develop the multiple intelligence's of students." Strategies include Gardner's Multiple Intelligences to make curriculum content more meaningful and accessible to students. The model uses social studies themes to help children develop as researchers and to work collaboratively in teams. DWoK's social studies themes help to establish the groundwork for meaningful educational partnerships between parents, school, and community. Plans are customized to solve real-world problems and the delivery of services by students is personalized to meet the needs of teachers, the school and the community.

DWoK focuses on helping students make connections across the curriculum. This is encouraged in regular interdisciplinary team meetings across grade levels. DWoK supports teachers' use of a variety of materials and strategies to create "an effective learner-centered classroom." Schools surveyed wrote that they use textbooks very little if at all and, instead, use many materials, including ones from the home.

DWoK has multiple assessment goals and a multiple source of self-reflections to help students and teachers refine their learning. Children are guided to use their problem-solving and communication strategies to create group and individual projects that demonstrate their understanding of the content. The model believes that in addition to rigorous student assessment, an important kind of evaluation is self-evaluation and invites active, collaborative reflection by both teachers and students. Portfolios also offer opportunities for sensitive in-depth learning and teaching. The model ensures that students and teachers are continuously reflecting on the learning experience to evaluate what worked, what didn't work, and why.

Sources:

Catterall, J. S. (1995). *Different Ways of Knowing: 1991-94 longitudinal study of program effects on students and teachers*. Los Angeles, CA: University of California, Los Angeles.

Catterall, J. S., Dreyfus, J. P., & DeJarnette, K. G. (1995). *Different Ways of Knowing: 1994-95 evaluation report*. Los Angeles, CA: University of California, Los Angeles.

Herman, R. (1999). *An educator's guide to schoolwide reform*. Retrieved 2002, from http://www.aasa.org/issues_and_insights/district_organization/Reform/index.htm.

Hovda, R., & Kyle, D. (1997). *Different Ways of Knowing: Effects on elementary teaching and learning practices*. Louisville, KY: University of Louisville.

Northwest Regional Educational Laboratory (2001). *The catalog of school reform models*. Retrieved 2002, from http://www.nwrel.org/scpd/catalog/index.shtml.

Wong, K., & Sogin, D. (1997). *Different Ways of Knowing: Effects on elementary teaching and learning practices*. Lexington, KY: University of Kentucky.

DIRECT INSTRUCTION

Association for Direct Instruction
P.O. Box 10252, Eugene, OR 97440, 541-485-1293, 541-683-7543
http://www.adihome.org

Score: Compatible

"We assumed that children were logical, reasonable beings in terms of how they responded to our teaching, and that their behavior was the ultimate judge of the effectiveness of whatever went into our teaching. If the way we taught didn't induce the desired learning, we hadn't taught it. But if children learned stuff that was wrong, we were responsible for that, too, and it meant we had to revise what we were doing and try it out again. That's the formula we used from the beginning."
– Siegfried E. Engelmann

Features:

♦ A scripted, back-to-basics curricular program for Pre-K-6.

♦ A skills-oriented process emphasizing the use of small groups of children, face-to-face, with teachers and aides who follow scripted lessons in which cognitive skills are broken down into small units. Mastery of the small units by students is necessary before moving on to more complex curriculum.

♦ Detailed developed lessons allow teachers to learn the Direct Instruction design theory as they teach.

♦ Lesson are field tested and updated before they are published.

Background: Direct Instruction (DI) was designed by Siegfried "Ziggy" Engelmann of the University of Oregon. The oldest version of the program, Distar, was developed in the 1960s as part of *Project Follow Through*, a major educational initiative of President Johnson's War on Poverty. The Association for Direct Instruction, a nonprofit organization is home to the model and provides support for educators using DI programs. The Association produces a professional quarterly magazine called *Effective School Practices*.

Premise: Children will generalize their learning to new examples and situations if they can respond perfectly to a smaller set of carefully engineered tasks. The model developer believes

that children learn best by working through the sequence of tasks with carefully timed comments from the teacher. Lessons are carefully tested and scripted. Scripting reduces "teacher talk" which according to the developer decreases student motivation, causes confusion by changing the focus of the tasks, and disrupts the development of the lesson.

Design: DI strives to accelerate the learning of at-risk students in grades Pre-K-6 through an instructional approach with curriculum materials and sequences that attempt to move students to mastery as quickly as possible. The model incorporates professional development and management for schools to optimize use of the design. Through training and in-class coaching, teachers in the lower grades learn to present highly interactive lessons to small groups. Under the DI program, students are encouraged to answer orally as much as possible, and teachers monitor and correct errors immediately. Students are placed at instructional levels based on performance, so those who need additional assistance receive it and those who learn rapidly are not held back. The model allows for inclusion of students with special needs except in the most extreme cases.

Two examples of the DI curriculum are:

Language for Learning for grades Pre-K-2. Through this curriculum, children learn the concepts, language rules, forms of communication, and classroom skills needed for oral and written expression, and for participation in school activities. The curriculum has 150 lessons organized into six groups of skills: Actions, Description of Objects, Information and Background Knowledge, Instructional Words and Problem-Solving Concepts, Classification, and Problem-Solving Strategies and Applications. The content of each of the six groups, with the exception of Classification, is divided into strands that continue across the lessons and are taught in an arranged sequence of exercises. Students apply what they have learned in earlier strands to the exercises in later tracks.

The *Reading Mastery* curriculum is broken down into fundamental elements including decoding and comprehension skills. Complex skills are taught in sequences of less complex skills that have been mastered. Lessons are taught in small groups, at a brisk pace, encouraging a high rate of student response, group and individual turns, and immediate correction to prevent the development of gaps in students' knowledge. Books are selected to provide both classical and modern fiction, history, poetry, geography, meteorology, and oceanography. The program strives to complete six years of reading instruction in five years.

DI is available for math and other subject areas. Trained classroom paraprofessionals are integrated into the program and work as instructional aides, one-on-one tutors, or small group leaders under the direction of certified teachers. The DI program includes a set of instructional materials published by SRA/ McGraw Hill in reading, remedial reading, spelling, math, writing, and language.

Evidence of Results: The American Institutes for Research's *An Educator's Guide to Schoolwide Reform* rated the model as having "strong evidence of positive effects on student achievement." This rating indicates that four or more studies, using rigorous methodologies, show positive effects of the model's approach on student achievement, "with at least three of such studies showing effects that are statistically significant."

A 2001 Wisconsin Policy Research Report on DI investigated the results of the DI program on students and teachers in six Wisconsin schools and found that this approach to teaching produced positive results. Teachers and principals reported positive results from DI in reading achievement and other areas.

In a suburban school, 'intervention' children (children who are behind in reading) and others showed strong improvements on the state's third-grade test of reading, with more than 90 percent attaining 'proficient' or 'advanced' scores. A Milwaukee school (the 27th Street School) registered the highest schoolwide increase in the district (from 1997 to 1999/00, on Wisconsin's fourth-grade Knowledge and Concepts exam), with a jump from 23 percent to 72 percent in children reading at the 'proficient' level or higher.

Compatibility with Service-Learning: The model scored itself as *compatible* with service-learning. The developer reports that flexible use of time is required for the model to work in the school, stating "There may be a need to do double language arts periods or increased math instruction." Flexible use of time is a great benefit to educators who would embark on a service-learning activity.

According to the model developer's answers to the survey, "A good DI teacher also creates additional activities that allow students to make use of their learning in various situations." Classroom projects (which could include service-learning projects if a school were inclined in this direction) are part of the curriculum.

Within the context of the curriculum, there are choices students must make, so the model does allow students to play a small role in planning curricular activities, an attribute found in quality service-learning. Local community needs are addressed as schools link projects to academic performance. For their "extension projects" students perform presentations to large groups within the school community. The model does encourage alternative assessment such as student presentations and time for student reflections is given "as appropriate."

Although the overall survey score for the model was *compatible*, the model scored as highly compatible in the following service-learning elements: providing opportunities for students to apply their knowledge or skills to real-life situations; adjusting curriculum to address local community needs; providing objectives for developing civic skills and competencies; and allowing students to play a role in planning curricular activities.

Sources:

American Federation of Teachers (1998). *Six promising schoolwide programs for raising student achievement. Direct Instruction.* Retrieved 2002, from http://www.aft.org/edissues/ whatworks/six/di/index.htm.

Clowes, G. A. (2001). If the children aren't learning, we're not teaching. An interview with Siegfried E. Engelmann. Retrieved 2002, from http://www.heartland.org/education/jun01/ engelmann.htm.

Engelmann, S., & Osborn, J. (1999). Language for learning: Teacher's guide. Columbus, OH: SRA-McGraw-Hill.

Herman, R. (1999). *An educator's guide to schoolwide reform.* Retrieved 2002, from http:// www.aasa.org/issues_and_insights/ district_organization/Reform/index.htm.

Schug, M., Tarver, S. G., & Western, R.D. (2001). Direct Instruction and the teaching of early reading. Wisconsin's teacher-led insurgency. *Wisconsin Policy Research Report, 14* (2).

EXPEDITIONARY LEARNING OUTWARD BOUND

100 Mystery Point Road, Garrison, NY 10524, 845-424-4000, 845-424-4280 fax
http://www.elob.org

Score: Highly Compatible

"We saw the power of planning an expedition around the reading process, with a strong focus on pre-reading and post-reading activities. By embedding writing in every facet of the expedition, we realized that the expedition and literacy goals are synergistic, not mutually exclusive." – *Suzanne Plaut, Christina Patterson, and Joseph Zaremba, teachers, The Harbor School, Boston, Massachusetts*

Features:

♦ Emphasis on learning by doing.

♦ Focus on building character, teamwork, and literacy, and connecting academic learning to adventure, service, and character development.

♦ Inter-connected, real-world projects called learning expeditions help teachers improve their ability to teach reading, writing, science, math, and other subjects.

♦ Literary instruction integrated into learning expeditions.

Background: Outward Bound originated in Great Britain and was founded by educator Kurt Hahn in 1941. Outward Bound courses were originally developed to prepare British merchant seamen to survive at sea and to rescue others.

Premise: Learning and growth occur through interaction among individuals accepting a challenge in an unfamiliar environment; and this learning transfers to meeting today's complex challenges at school or work.

Design: Expeditionary Learning Outward Bound, a model for elementary, middle, and high school emphasizes the philosophy of learning by doing. A multi-year professional development plan with instructional materials and technical assistance ushers in changes in culture, structures, teaching practices, and raises student achievement.

The underpinnings of the model are its five core practices.

1. *Learning Expeditions*: Long-term, in-depth investigations of a topic that engages students through authentic projects, fieldwork, and service.

2. *Reflection and Critique*: Teachers model a culture of reflection, critique, revision, and collaboration. This assessment allows teachers to discover what students know and how they learn. Specific protocols help teachers improve their craft.

3. *School Culture*: Through shared beliefs and practices, schools develop a strong culture of best effort, high expectations, community, collaboration, service, and diversity.

4. *School Structures*: Reorganization of instructional time into longer and more flexible blocks, student grouping, and resources are needed to support high quality learning expeditions. Multiyear teaching (students stay with the same teacher or team of teachers for more than one year) strengthens relationships and improves the likelihood of academic success.

5. *School Review*: Annual cycle of reflection, planning, and action to improve quality of teaching and learning.

Learning expeditions are hands-on studies of single topics such as the Civil Rights Movement, water quality, or the scientific revolution. These studies are long-term and last between three and six months, featuring in-depth projects and final performances before authentic audiences that may include family and community members. Teachers plan the learning expeditions alone or with a group of teachers, using topics, questions, and goals informed by district and state standards. Regular assessment, revision and constant improvement of student work is also a part of the learning expedition study.

Expeditionary Learning teaches a specific protocol that helps discussion and critique of instructional practice. Teacher study groups promote inquiry and innovation in classroom practice. Students are encouraged to share their ideas in a safe and supportive environment. Both teachers and students use portfolio assessment to drive student performance. The model believes that work that is placed in the student portfolio has reached a level of excellence and offers some of the best evidence of what students know and are able to do. A student's portfolio, the model believes, can also reveal the level of teaching practice a student is exposed to.

According to the developer, a school using Expeditionary Learning will see its school culture transformed by a "conscious application of the design principles, that are evident throughout the school in the way people treat one another and in every aspect of teaching and learning." The model guides schools to promote a school culture that exudes respect, compassion, and is engaging and physically and emotionally safe. Teachers in an Expeditionary Learning school appreciate the ideas of students, and encourage students to both pose and solve problems. Family members are also encouraged to play a role in shaping the school's culture.

Expeditionary Learning has created benchmarks for schools to use for conducting an initial assessment to find out where they stand at the beginning of the implementation of the design, and then as a yearly review. Schools develop a school review portfolio that gives a comprehensive picture of students', teachers', and leadership's performance and growth. The benchmarks provide a guide for reflection, planning and action for continuous improvement schoolwide. They help the school develop a

shared vision, look at change as a developmental process, set priorities, decide what evidence to collect and analyze, and develop a comprehensive evidence-driven school improvement plan.

The model's design also calls for the school to conduct a Periodic Peer Review to record and showcase their performance. Judged by an external evaluator, this review gives the school an unbiased perspective on its progress. The periodic peer review follows after the school's annual self-review and should focus on student learning and teaching practice in the context of the model's benchmarks. Expeditionary Learning is quick to clarify that the peer review process is not an external evaluation that ranks the school, but rather a review by critical friends who share similar goals in their own schools. The process allows the school to get an outsider's view and then reflect, revise, and improve.

Evidence of Results: Six independent organizations and researchers including American Institutes for Research, the National Staff Development Council, Academy for Educational Development, University of Colorado Department of Education, RAND Corporation, and researcher Polly Ulichny of Brown University concluded that Expeditionary Learning: "brings about significant improvements in student achievement as measured by standardized tests and portfolios of student work; changes instructional practices and school culture for the better; improves student attendance and parent participation; and reduces the need for disciplinary action."

In a report issued by New American Schools in 1997, early indicators of progress showed recognition for schools using Expeditionary Learning. Midway Elementary School was one of five schools chosen for an Excellence in Education Award presented by the Cincinnati Youth Collaborative in 1996-97. Three other Expeditionary Learning schools in the district were among the finalists chosen out of 79 schools competing. In Maine, an Expeditionary Learning school, King Middle School in Portland, achieved dramatic gains on the Maine Educational Assessment in six curriculum areas in 1995. In New York City, a three-year longitudinal comparison showed increases in reading on the Degrees of Reading Power Test in grades seven and eight, ranked the School for the Physical City at 29th among 226 junior high schools in the city in reading. These are a few of the examples cited in the New American Schools report.

Compatibility with Service-Learning: The model scored itself as *highly compatible* with service-learning and provides substantial support for service-learning activities or projects. Block scheduling is a key structure needed for learning expeditions. Student input is a central feature. According to the developer, "Expeditions are usually designed by teachers with student choice and planning as a natural component–the spirit of adventure."

The model's *Ten Design Principles* are highly compatible with service-learning: The Primacy of Self-Discovery, The Having of Wonderful Ideas, The Responsibility for Learning, Intimacy and Caring, Success and Failure, Collaboration and Competition, Diversity and Inclusively, The Natural World, Solitude and Reflection, and Service and Compassion.

In the model's *Five Core Principles*, "our best statement for bringing together the academic aspects of schooling with civic skills," service is specifically mentioned. The design also publishes safe fieldwork guidelines to ease district concerns over student safety during a learning expedition. "We do not provide a curriculum. We do discuss practices," wrote the developer.

The concept of students applying their knowledge and skills to real-life situations, problems, or projects, is a central feature of the model's design. One school surveyed wrote, "Students produce projects at the end of each expedition, then present them to parents, visitors, and/or appropriate city or state personnel."
The model addresses community needs in its design principles and *Community Practices*

Benchmarks. "We develop things that the community needs or has an interest in," wrote one school. Students are encouraged to participate in choosing expedition ideas and planning activities, but most of the planning rests on the teacher. In developing expeditions, teachers are encouraged to use research books, maps from City Hall and information gleaned from individuals. Teachers team teach and share duties during an expedition. Teachers use alternative forms of assessment such as rubrics and allow time for reflection and journal entries depending on the project or class.

Sources:
Cousins, E., & Mednic, A. (1999). *Service at the heart of learning: Teachers' writings*. Garrison, NY: Expeditionary Learning Outward Bound.

Kilmister, D., Liebowitz, M., & Udall, D. (1999). *Are we there yet? Benchmarks and tools for schools implementing Expeditionary Learning Outward Bound*. Garrison, NY: Expeditionary Learning Outward Bound.

Mednick, A., Wainwright, C., & Cousins, E. (2001). *Expeditionary Learning Outward Bound: A design for Comprehensive School Reform*. Garrison, NY: Expeditionary Learning Outward Bound.

New American High Schools Development Corporation (1997). *Working towards excellence: Results from schools implementing New American Schools designs*. Washington, D.C.

THE FOXFIRE FUND

P.O. Box 541, Mountain City, GA 30562, 706-746-5828, 706-746-5829 fax
http://www.foxfire.org

Score: Somewhat Compatible

"Classrooms should be dynamic learning sites where students and teachers work as partners to meet the goals of the curriculum." – *The Foxfire Fund*

Features:

♦ Student-centered, community-oriented, active learning.

♦ Incorporates Eleven Core Practices that capture the spirit of John Dewey's philosophy on how learning occurs.

♦ Student participation in planning.

♦ Curriculum integrated into the community.

♦ Teacher as facilitator of learning.

Background: The Foxfire Fund is an independent, non-profit organization founded in 1966 by Eliot Wigginton when local students at Rabun Gap-Nacooche School began recording the history of Southern Appalachia. Following in their footsteps, Foxfire students from Rabun County High School continued interviewing and photographing people in Southern Appalachia, documenting their crafts, skills, and way of life. The work was compiled and documented in *The Foxfire Magazine's* debut in March 1967 and eventually led to the publication of *The Foxfire Book* series. The teacher education program began in 1986.

Premise: Learner-centered and community-focused with clear connections to John Dewey's vision of experiential education.

Design: A Foxfire classroom is characterized as one that encompasses a dynamic learning environment with considerable student involvement and action, rigorous assessment and evaluation, reflection, imagination, and problem solving. Teachers and students work together to make decisions on how they will learn, and how

they will evaluate how well they have learned. Lines blur between the classroom and the community as teachers guide the learning experience beyond the classroom and out into the environment and the community.

The model does not consider itself a comprehensive school reform program, but rather, an educational framework and philosophy consisting of Eleven Core Practices of effective teaching and learning. The Core Practices, which show considerable compatibility with service-learning, continue to expand and evolve through Foxfire training sessions and network activities.

The Core Practices are:

1. The work teachers and learners do together is infused from the beginning with learner choice, design, and revision.

2. The role of the teacher is that of facilitator and collaborator.

3. The academic integrity of the work teachers and learners do together is clear.

4. The work is characterized by active learning.

5. Peer teaching, small group work, and teamwork are all consistent features of classroom activities.

6. Connections between classroom work, surrounding communities, and the world beyond the community are clear.

7. There is an audience beyond the teacher for viewing student work.

8. New activities spiral gracefully out of the old, incorporating lessons learned from past experiences, building on skills and understandings that can now be amplified.

9. Imagination and creativity are encouraged in the completion of learning activities.

10. Reflection is an essential activity that takes place at key points throughout the work.

11. The work teachers and learners do together includes rigorous, ongoing assessment and evaluation.

John Dewey's philosophy of education flows through the Foxfire model–all genuine education comes through experience, the teacher should be a co-partner and guide in a common enterprise, the child's education as an independent learner and thinker, and there should be a natural connection between the school and the community. Other Dewey theories on aspects of education, including the relationships among teachers, learners, curriculum, and community; the ways learning occurs; preparing for lives as citizens and individuals; and thinking about what is learned and how, are described by the model developer as being the spirit of the Foxfire approach to teaching and learning.

The model's first five Core Practices focus on the relationship between the teacher and the student and how they work together on the student's educational goals. Through these Practices, the model addresses the student's voice, the teacher becomes a facilitator and collaborator, academic integrity of work done between student and teacher is clarified, and learning becomes active and is done in a team or small group.

The model integrates various progressive educational methods and ideas and supports a democratic classroom that connects students' learning to the community. This is seen in Core Practices 6 and 7, "Connections between the classroom work, the surrounding communities, and the world beyond the community are clear."

Core Practice 8 speaks to building upon lessons learned, or "spiraling." Dewey referred to this as "the continuous spiral," and stressed the need for activities to be linked cumulatively and logically so children can use lessons learned as a base for future experiences.

Foxfire encourages an active, learner-centered approach to education with meaningful and authentic ties to the real world. Core Practices 5 and 9 help students prepare to become engaged citizens. These practices expose students to a combination of teamwork, inclusion and creativity, skills that prepare students to be engaged in their community, working, and getting along with others.

Core Practice 10 introduces students to the concept of reflection and Core Practice 11 addresses evaluation and assessment. Creating an expectation of reflection or an environment that respects reflection helps teachers increase "the transfer of knowledge" and enables student to "engage in rigorous, ongoing assessment and evaluation." "Because these activities take place at key points during a study–rather than just at the completion –they evoke insight and give rise to revisions and refinements critical to improving learning and addressing accountability."

Three networks across the country operate as a local organization dedicated to the support of teachers who are using the Foxfire Approach. The networks provide seminars, group meetings, newsletters, and other services as part of their membership. Foxfire promotes a strong emphasis on the importance of teachers guiding their own development. They have pioneered their teachers-teaching-teachers professional development into the formation of a teachers' network, or fellowship. The model is deeply committed to teachers and their involvement as thinkers, planners, evaluators, and change agents.

Evidence of Results: No evidence of independent evaluation was found on the model.

Compatibility with Service-Learning: The model scored itself, surprisingly, as only *somewhat compatible* with service-learning. Although the model scored "not applicable" in the areas of the survey that referenced flexible use of time such as block scheduling, they do take advantage of block scheduling "when the opportunity arises." Foxfire's Dewey-based philosophy is highly compatible with the ideals of service-learning.

Connections between class work, the surrounding communities, and the world beyond the community are important in the model design. The spiraling and linking of learning activities cumulatively can be applied easily to a service-learning project or unit. The model's Core Practice 9 speaks directly to a service-learning key element, preparing students to become engaged citizens. The model allows students to play a role in planning curricular activities. "The work teachers and learners do is infused from the beginning with learner choice, design and revision." The model supports instructional methods that include project-based learning when appropriate.

Alternative assessments are addressed. According to Foxfire, "The work teachers and learners [students] do together includes rigorous, ongoing assessment and evaluation. Teachers and learners employ a variety of strategies to demonstrate their mastery of teaching and learning objectives." Reflection is integrated deeply into the model. "Reflection is an essential activity that takes place at key points throughout the work."

Sources:

National Commission on Teaching and America's Future (2000). *What matters most: Teaching for America's future.* Retrieved 2002, from http://www.tc.columbia.edu/nctaf/policy/networks.html.

Starnes, B. A. (1999). *The Foxfire approach to teaching and Learning: John Dewey, Experiential Learning, and the Core Practices.* Eric Digest, ERIC Clearninghouse on Rural Education and Small Schools Charleston, WV. ED426826.

Starnes, B., Paris, C., & Stevens, C. (1999). *The Foxfire core practices: Discussions and implications.* Mountain City, GA: Foxfire.

HIGH SCHOOLS THAT WORK

Southern Regional Education Board
592 10th St. N.W., Atlanta, GA 30318-5790, 404-875-9211, 404-872-1477 fax
http://sreb.org/programs/hstw/hstwindex.asp

Score: Compatible

"Most students can master complex academic and technical concepts if schools create an environment that encourages students to make the effort to succeed." – *Gene Bottoms*

Features:

- Upgraded academic core with a concentration in further academic studies or a career/technical field.

- Use of engaging instructional strategies, including applied and contextual learning.

- Includes data collection and evaluation to drive the reform process at schools.

Background: High Schools That Work (HSTW) was created in 1987 by the Southern Regional Education Board–State Vocational Education Consortium. Gene Bottoms, Senior Vice President of Southern Regional Education Board (SREB), is the founding director of HSTW.

Premise: Teaching a more intellectually challenging curriculum to career-oriented students is based on five elements: 1) greater effort by students; 2) a challenging program of study that blends essential content from college-preparatory studies with quality career/technical studies; 3) quality work by all students; 4) support for learning, including guidance/advisement and extra help; and 5) use of data to guide school improvement.

Design: The model combines strong academic preparation with a concentration in an academic area or a modern career/technical field in preparing all high school students for the workplace and further education. It provides a framework of goals, key practices, and key conditions for setting higher standards and

accelerating learning. SREB advocates that all students complete an upgraded academic core, taught to college-preparatory standards, and four credits in a concentration in either a broad career/technical field of study or further academic studies, such as mathematics/science or humanities. The intent is to get all high school students to focus on a group of challenging and related courses that interest and prepare them for the future.

The HSTW design is driven by three core goals:

1. Raise the mathematics, science, communication, problem-solving, and technical achievement of students to the national average and above.

2. Blend the essential content of traditional college-preparatory studies–mathematics, science, and English language arts–with quality career/technical studies by creating conditions that support school leaders, teachers, and counselors in carrying out key practices.

3. Advance state and local policies and leadership initiatives necessary to sustain a continuous school-improvement effort.

Ten key practices are the essence of the HSTW design:

1. High expectations.

2. Challenging career/technical studies.

3. Academic studies teaching essential concepts from the college-preparatory curriculum

and encouraging students to use academic content and skills to address real-world projects and problems.

4. A challenging program of study that includes a solid academic core and a concentration.

5. Work-based learning.

6. Teachers working together–integrated instruction.

7. Students actively engaged in learning.

8. Guidance and advisement.

9. Extra help in meeting higher standards.

10. Marking progress by using assessment and evaluation data to improve school and classroom practices.

SREB works with a number of stakeholders in the HSTW reform process. Local superintendents, principals, teachers, counselors, school board members, business and postsecondary leaders, and representatives of state departments of education are consulted early and often in the implementation of the model. Stakeholders agree to fully implement HSTW goals, key practices, and key conditions in member schools. In return, the schools receive staff development, technical assistance, publications and communications, and data and evaluation services from SREB and state departments of education.

SREB promotes the use of contextual learning strategies to show students how to apply abstract ideas in a variety of real-life situations. Academic and career/technical teachers work together to develop assignments that encourage students to use challenging academic knowledge and skills to complete projects and solve open-ended problems based on real-world applications. Integrating college-preparatory academic studies with career/technical studies gives students more options for learning complex reading, writing, mathematics, and science concepts. "Contextual learning does not take the effort out of learning," Bottoms wrote. "Rather, it creates a climate in which learning is taken seriously and students help each other

succeed." The use of contextual learning demonstrates significant compatibility with service-learning.

High Schools That Work prepares teachers to use effective instructional methods. The topics, following, for national and site-specific professional development include many that are compatible with service-learning.

- Reading and writing for learning across the curriculum.

- Aligning teacher assignments, student work, and assessments.

- Analyzing "power standards" to determine what students need to know and be able to do, and moving standards into instruction.

- Using project-based learning.

- Using real-world problems to engage students in learning algebra and geometry.

- Using cooperative learning strategies.

- Improving student-centered instruction.

- Training teachers as advisors.

- Planning and implementing ninth-grade catch-up academies.

- Training teachers to use The College Board's Pacesetter English in grades nine and 12 and Pacesetter Mathematics in grade 12.

- Integrating mathematics and reading into career/technical courses.

- Implementing career academies in grades 10 through 12.

- Creating a climate of higher expectations.

- Integrating technology into classroom instruction.

SREB urges HSTW sites to mount schoolwide literacy and numeracy initiatives to raise the reading, writing, and mathematics skills of all students, including career-oriented students. The schools identify literacy and numeracy "coaches," who are trained by SREB to work with teachers in improving students' English language arts and mathematics skills through year-round instructional activities in every classroom.

Staff Development–HSTW plans and conducts meetings, workshops, and conferences to help schools find solutions to common problems. The staff development includes national workshops for administrators, teachers, and counselors; retreats and institutes for local and state leaders; and Internet courses. More than 6,000 educators participate in the annual HSTW Staff Development Conference–a showcase for new and successful ideas and approaches.

Technical Assistance–HSTW organizes teams to conduct technical assistance visits to one-third of the HSTW sites each year. The purpose of the visits is to help schools determine their progress, their challenges and their next steps in improving student achievement. Each visit results in a no-nonsense report of actions the school can consider to advance student learning.

Communications and Publications–HSTW produces many publications annually and maintains a catalog of HSTW policy reports, research briefs, case studies, site development guides, outstanding practices publications, and videotapes to assist schools in raising student achievement. Regular mailings contain newsletters and other materials needed by the sites. The SREB Web page contains a large section of news and information about HSTW and its network of states and sites.

Assessment–All HSTW sites participate in the initiative's biennial assessment of reading, mathematics, and science achievement. The assessment is based on the National Assessment of Educational Progress (NAEP). Sites also participate in the HSTW Teacher Survey and the Follow-up Study of recent graduates who report on their high school experiences. HSTW conducts a transcript study to match students' course-taking patterns with their performance on the assessment. HSTW schools use data from the initiative and from other sources to measure

their progress in raising student achievement. Sites are expected to use a number of indicators to measure their progress and to make steady advances in improving student learning.

Curriculum products–HSTW trains teachers to use valid curriculum products that address what and how students are taught. Pacesetter Mathematics and Pacesetter English are part of a College Board program that integrates standards, curriculum, teacher development and assessment. Principles of Technology is a two-year contextual physics curriculum that focuses on using physics to solve real-life problems. Project Lead The Way is a project-based pre-engineering curriculum that incorporates college-preparatory mathematics and science in grades nine through 12.

Evidence of Results: External research reports by national organizations have shown the impact of HSTW in helping schools improve curriculum instruction and student performance. The American Institutes for Research selected HSTW in 1999 as the nation's only high school reform initiative that shows "strong evidence" of raising student performance. The Research Triangle Institute prepared a study on HSTW for the U.S. Department of Education. This study showed that HSTW schools in a two-year period were able to increase the percentages of students who met the HSTW achievement goals and completed the recommended program of study. MPR Associates Inc. found gains in student achievement linked to HSTW key practices, particularly an upgraded academic core, integrated academic and career/technical studies, and guidance/advisement about educational and career plans.

Compatibility with Service Learning: The model scored itself as *compatible* with service-learning. SREB considers service-learning to be a form of work-based learning. More than two-thirds of all high school students work during their senior year. Quality work-based learning experiences are associated with higher academic achievement. The five experiences that SREB recommends for students engaged in work-based learning are: 1) observing veteran workers in certain jobs; 2) learning how to do a job from a work-site mentor; 3) being evaluated according to clear standards; 4) receiving encouragement from a work-site mentor at least monthly to develop strong work habits and good customer relations skills; and 5) being shown daily or weekly how to use communication skills at the work site. HSTW students who have all or some of these quality work-based learning experiences are more likely than other students to meet the HSTW achievement goals in reading, mathematics, and science.

SREB encourages HSTW schools to use grade 12 as a time for students to combine their knowledge and skills in a Senior Project to show what they have learned in academic and career/technical courses. A Senior Project combines a written research report, a product or service to the community, and an oral report to a panel of experts in a career/technical field. A number of HSTW schools and school districts value the Senior Project enough to make it a requirement for graduation.

Sources:

High Schools That Work, Home Page
www.sreb.org/programs/hstw/hstwindex.asp.

Bottoms, G. (1998). *Things that matter most in improving student learning*. Atlanta, GA: Southern Regional Education Board.

Bottoms, G. (2000). *Putting lessons learned to work: Improving the achievement of vocational students*. Atlanta, GA: Southern Regional Education Board.

Bottoms, G. (2000). *The 2000 High Schools That Work assessment: Improving urban high schools*. Atlanta, GA: Southern Regional Education Board.

Bottoms, G., & O'Neill, K. (2001). *Preparing a new breed of school principals: It's time for action*. Atlanta, GA: Southern Regional Education Board.

Bottoms, G., & Sharpe, D. (1996). *Teaching for understanding through integration of academic and technical education*. Atlanta, GA: Southern Regional Education Board.

Frome, P. (April 2001). *High Schools That Work: Findings from the 1996 and 1998 assessments*. Prepared by Research Triangle Institute for Planning and Evaluation Service, U.S. Department of Education. Retrieved 2002, from http://www.sreb.org/programs/hstw/ResearchReports/findings_from_assessment.asp.

Herman, R. (Project Director) (1999). *An educator's guide to schoolwide reform*. Retrieved 2002, from http://www.aasa.org/issues_and_insights/district_organization/Reform/index.htm

Kaufman, P., Bradby, D., & Teitelbaum, P. (2000). *High Schools That Work and whole school reform: Raising academic achievement of vocational completers through the reform of school practice*. MPR Associates Inc. and National Center for Research in Vocational Education, University of California at Berkeley: Berkeley, CA.

Southern Regional Education Board (2001). *Closing the achievement gap: A High Schools That Work design for challenged schools*. Atlanta, GA: Author.

Southern Regional Education Board (Fall 2001). *Literacy across the curriculum*. *High Schools That Work*. Update Newsletter

Southern Regional Education Board (2001). *HSTW presents a pre-engineering program of study*. Atlanta, GA: Author.

Southern Regional Education Board (2002). High Schools That Work: new partnerships and a national network to improve high school education, revised edition. Atlanta, GA: Author.

Southern Regional Education Board (2002). Senior project guide: *Students develop academic and technical skills by writing a research report, producing a product and making and oral presentation*. Atlanta, GA: Author.

HIGH/SCOPE® PRIMARY GRADES

Approach to Education
600 North River St., Ypsilanti, MI 48198, 734-485-2000, 734-485-0704 fax
http:www.highscope.org

Score: Compatible

"The capacities that students develop in a High/Scope classroom are broad abilities that they can and do use daily in classrooms or at home and that are carried into their adult lives."
– *Art Stellar, High/Scope President and CEO*

Features:
- Set of guiding principles and practices for teachers to adapt to the special needs and conditions of students, the setting of the educational environment, and the community.

- Pre-K-3 activities include training for elementary teachers and administrators; conducting research projects; developing curricula for infant/toddler, pre-school, elementary, and adolescent programs; publishing books, videos, and curricular materials; and operating a residential enrichment program for adolescents.

- Active learning is key.

Background: The High/Scope Foundation is an independent research, development, training, and public advocacy organization located in Ypsilanti, Michigan, founded in 1970 by David P. Weikart. The curriculum originated from one of the first early childhood intervention programs of the 1960s, the High/Scope Perry Preschool Project, and was further developed with funding as a demonstration project in the First Chance Network for handicapped preschoolers.

Premise: Children learn best though active experiences with people, materials, events and ideas, rather than through direct teaching or sequenced exercises. Based on education philosophers like John Dewey, Jean Piaget, and Lev Vygotsky, the model supports students' individual state of development, interests, and innate predisposition to learning. The model calls its approach both progressive and cognitive-developmental.

Design: This is not a whole school model. The High/Scope Primary Grades Approach to Education focuses on young students and touches on all curriculum areas. The design includes small group instruction, active learning, learning centers, observational and portfolio assessment, technology integration, and other materials. Parents and the community are encouraged to become actively involved in workshops and in the classroom. The model recommends that schools get students to initiate their own learning activities.

Within an open framework, teachers design a classroom program guided by the needs and interests of the children being served. The High/Scope approach has the teacher identify each child and rank them on a developmental continuum by examining their strengths and accomplishments. High/Scope views discrepancies in behavior as developmental delays, not as deficiencies. This also applies in respect to children with disabilities and their peers. Teachers initiate developmentally appropriate experiences that reflect long-range educational goals.

The model's cyclical *Plan-Do-Review* sequence encourages children to achieve these goals by involving them in decision-making and problem-solving situations throughout the day. The teacher serves as a learning facilitator and encourages students to extend learning beyond the current lesson at hand.

The following is an example of *Plan-Do-Review* for early elementary found on the AskEric

Virtual Library in a teacher-to-teacher communication.

> *... we often applied the "Plan-Do-Review" process to the activities within a project. Some examples:*
>
> *Studying rocks–*Plan*: Gather rocks and use a testing system to determine their contents.* Do*: Collecting and actual testing.* Review*: Was this effective? How can we show what we've learned? And then ...* Plan*: How to display the information gathered.* Do*: Creating the display.* Review*: Did we teach others? Was the information interesting and understood?*
>
> *Studying Animals–*Plan*: Which animals should we study and how should we get information about them?* Do*: Reading books, visiting a store or zoo, or having an expert visit.* Review*: What did we learn? And then ...* Plan*: Let's make an alligator.* Do*: (Now here you may get into sub-plan-do reviews, i.e., how to make, testing materials, making a diagram or plan for construction)* Review*: Does it look the way we wanted it to? What did we learn from doing this?*
>
> *...High/Scope provides a framework for organizing project work–maybe a disposition on how to organize your ideas and goals. Eventually it becomes almost second nature to the students.*
> *– Bridget M. Budde, teacher*

Teachers maintain a daily routine that permits children to learn actively. The model suggests arranging instructional activity centers inside the classroom to facilitate learning experiences in math, language, science, art, social studies, movement, and music, and matching children's needs with appropriate content, skills, and concepts. Teachers join in the children's activities and ask questions that extend their plans and thinking. Daily, small-group instructional workshops are organized to involve concepts and skills in major content areas, engaging children in key development experiences that will help them learn to make choices and solve problems.

The model provides training designed to give teachers concrete strategies and information that they can take back to their classrooms, such as a child observation assessment technique. Short and in-depth training programs prepare participants to achieve full implementation of the High/Scope educational approach in their classrooms or centers, or to train others in the High/Scope active learning approach.

Evidence of Results: In a study comparing achievement test scores of children in High/Scope classrooms at three elementary schools to children in non-High/Scope classrooms, over a three-year period, significant advantages in favor of the High/Scope children were found. Out of a total of 40 composite score comparisons (including reading, language, mathematics, science, and social studies on the Comprehensive Test of Basic Skills, the Iowa Test of Basic Skills, and the California Achievement Tests), at the three sites, the High/Scope groups scored significantly higher.

Researchers from the Stanford Research Institute in Menlo Park, California found higher levels of child initiative and goal-directed child activity in High/Scope than in non-High/Scope classrooms. Students had richer vocabularies and wrote longer, more descriptive and effective reports. A year after leaving a High/Scope classroom, students more frequently initiated reading and writing activities and had better attitudes toward reading and writing.

According to W.S. Barnett's 1996 study, *Lives in the Balance*, that looked at the lives of 123 at-risk African Americans ages 3 and 4, in the 1960s, who received a high-quality preschool program on High/Scope's active learning approach, results revealed that by age 27, these youth fared better than a control group for arrest rates, earnings, economic status, educational performance, and commitment to marriage. With those positive results, Barnett found that the High/Scope Preschool program produced a net saving of $7.16 for every dollar invested.

Compatibility with Service-Learning: The model developer scored High/Scope as *compatible* with service-learning. High/Scope allows for opportunities for students to apply their knowledge and skills to real-life situations, problems, or projects in the *Plan-Do-Review* process. According to the developer, this process allows children, with the help of their teacher, to initiate plans for projects or activities, work in learning centers to implement their plans, then review what they have accomplished with teachers and classmates. One school wrote that the model, "Promotes active learning, hands-on developmentally appropriate practice via the workshop model and the *Plan-Do-Review* approach."

The model's approach builds in numerous opportunities for children to engage in social processes with friends, family, and community. The *Plan-Do-Review* approach, according to one school surveyed, "requires student initiative in planning." Another school wrote, "*Plan-Do-Review* allows children to demonstrate, perform, or illustrate their knowledge, performance, and understanding."

The model's approach is designed to foster self-confidence and social competence in all children–skills that are necessary to function in today's society where teamwork and problem solving are increasingly important. "The High/Scope program encourages child-initiated learning experiences that enable children to interact cooperatively and productively with classmates and teachers. High/Scope activity centers are stocked with a variety of supplies, manipulative materials, and equipment to provide a learning environment that encourages active manipulation and formulation of practical problems," wrote the developer. Hands-on active learning, integrated curriculum, and performance-based standards were listed by one school as examples of teaching strategies used in with design that are compatible with service-learning. Assessments used include standards-based performances, portfolios, presentations, and projects.

The model promotes a daily schedule that provides frequent opportunities for children to work with materials and equipment as they devise projects of their own choosing or through teacher assigned tasks.

By promoting the model's instructional goals while simultaneously supporting the child's personal interest, ideas, and abilities, teachers encourage students to become enthusiastic participants in the active learning process. High/Scope teachers document and assess students' progress through two primary methods: by collecting brief anecdotal notes that record observations of students' behaviors and compiling collections of student work samples. Students' reflection is an integral part of the daily *Plan-Do-Review* process, which is the hallmark of High/Scope active learning process.

Sources:
High/Scope, Home Page http://www.highscope.org/.

Barnett, W. S. (1996). *Lives in the balance: Age-27 benefit-cost analysis of the High/Scope Perry Preschool Program* (Monographs of the High/Scope Educational Research Foundation, 11). Ypsilanti, MI: High/Scope Press.

Northwest Regional Educational Laboratory (2001). *The catalog of school reform models*. Retrieved 2002, from http://www.nwrel.org/scpd/catalog/index.shtml.

U. S. Department of Education (1995). *Educational programs that work: The catalogue of the National Diffusion Network*, 21st Edition. Retrieved 2002, from http://www.ed.gov/pubs/EPTW/eptw11/.

INTEGRATED THEMATIC INSTRUCTION

17051 SE 272nd Street, Suite 17, Kent, WA 98042, 253-631-4400, 253-631-7500 fax
http://www.kovalik.com

Score: Highly Compatible

"Being able to put knowledge to real world use sparked my interest in brain research. In studying brain research, I came to realize that everyone is capable of learning and excelling."
– *Susan Kovalik*

Features:

♦ Cutting-edge research on how the brain learns is applied to the model's approach to instructional practice, teaching strategies, and curriculum.

♦ Considered an appropriate model for whole school, whole district, and whole state.

Background: Model developer Susan Kovalik's background in education and grounding in brain research prompted her to create the Integrated Thematic Instruction (ITI) model, in the early 1980s, for implementing body-brain compatible learning. Her work has spread beyond the United States to Slovakia. As a result of her work in Slovakia, there are now over 20 "teacher learning" centers and two colleges certifying ITI teachers. Kovalik's leadership has led many educators to see that the biology of learning is a vital foundation for making decisions that take learning to higher levels.

Premise: Current knowledge about brain research has inspired an examination of traditional practices in education, challenging educators to drop what is ineffective and embrace promising new approaches that are compatible with what we know about how the brain develops and learns. Scientists now know the brain is built before and after birth and that one's experience literally shapes one's brain for survival. Kovalik's ITI model focuses on "conceptual understanding of content, basic skills and the foresight to know when to use them, the ability to apply what is learned to real world situations, capability to work collaboratively with others, and a vision of themselves as contributing members of society."

Design: The ITI model is a K-12 program that applies current brain research to teaching strategies and curriculum to develop educated and responsible citizens. The model has a year-long theme integrated into the curriculum that includes an enriched school and classroom environment, guidelines for life skills, and learning that is tied to locations and issues in the community. The design reduces the need for pull-out programs, provides longer blocks of instructional time, and recommends common planning time for educators. Parents are provided with training and may be included as resource speakers and ITI school site hosts.

Integrated Thematic Instruction (ITI) brings three independent areas of best knowledge and practice together to form the core structure of its design. These are:

1. Research on the biology of learning. The model translated current knowledge of the biology of learning into practical application and implements nine "bodybrain-compatible" elements:

   a. Absence of Threat
   b. Meaningful Content
   c. Choices
   d. Movement to Enhance Learning
   e. Adequate Time
   f. Enriched Environment
   g. Collaboration
   h. Immediate Feedback
   i. Mastery (application level)

2. Teaching strategies that align with the way the human brain learns have the greatest impact. The model designed the physical classroom to support long-term learning in order to create workable teams of students and develop classroom management that uses agreements, procedures, *Lifelong Guidelines* and *LIFESKILLS* principles. Research-based strategies, such as cooperative learning, are also used.

3. *Curriculum development by teachers makes learning come alive.* Teachers anchor the curriculum to a year-long theme and rationale. The curriculum is aligned to district and state standards and orchestrates "being there" experiences tied to meaningful content and outreach to the community.

The ITI model begins with an understanding of five learning principles derived from bodybrain research:

1. Intelligence is a function of experience.

2. Learning is an inseparable partnership between brain and body:

   a. Emotions are the gatekeepers to learning and performance.

   b. Movement enhances learning.

3. There are multiple intelligences or ways for solving problems and producing products.

4. Learning is a two-step process:

   a. Step one: Making meaning through pattern seeking.

   b. Step two: Developing a mental program for using what we understand and wiring it into long-term memory.

5. Personality impacts learning and performance.

The impact of emotion and experience on the brain's ability to learn is described by Dr. Jane McGeehan, a former public school teacher, administrator, and currently chief executive officer of Susan Kovalik & Associates. In an article called "Brain-Compatible Learning," McGeenan quotes leading brain researchers who assert that "Emotion is the highest part of our mindbody survival kit," and "Emotions drive attention which drives learning, memory, and just about everything else." One of the key roles of emotion is to tell the brain what is worth attending to and the attitude with which one attends. When learning something, the body and brain are inseparable and interdependent. Based on the current research on the brain and how emotions are connected to learning, McGeehan contends that in classroom application, emotions are the gatekeepers to learning. Positive relationships among teachers and students, a predictable climate, common language describing the ways in which people agree to interact respectfully, and an environment of players who obviously care about each other are all important to learning. Activities that promote this, according to McGeehan, are ones that: build a sense of community by creating safe ways for students to say what they need and want, posting agendas so that students have a picture of what is coming, and teaching students constructive ways to resolve conflict and to encourage each other. This kind of environment puts the student in the best emotional state to allow them to focus full attention on learning.

Experience is important in brain development as well. Experiences that provide rich sensory input beyond the capacity of a textbook or worksheet promote growth and increased synaptic connections in the brain. McGeehan writes, "First-hand experiences in the world outside the school and with real things inside the school evoke such rich sensory input to the brain. Visiting the pond, inspecting an earthworm up close, observing a seed become a plant–these are the experiences that enhance neural networks. Learning that starts with a 'being-there' experience gives added power to all other kinds of input whether it be immersion, hands-on with real objects, with models, second hand, or symbolic."

The ITI curriculum, focuses on developing student understanding of important concepts, such as change, through a curriculum that begins with a location or event in the student's world. Students are led by the teacher to investigate and conduct research to answer questions, such as: "What's going on around here?" "So what?" and "Why do we have to learn this?" The model trains teachers to ask themselves guiding questions such as, "What do I want students to do with their understanding that leads to responsible citizenship?" Community locations or events are the starting point for curriculum integration. Students might visit a hospital, a playground, a waste treatment plant, a local park, or a retirement home. Bringing students to a location to allow them a "being there" experience provides the foundation for powerful learning where the integration of a unit of study occurs naturally and makes sense.

Curriculum is written with assessment in mind. Teachers provide examples of good work for students to see and rubrics to encourage self-assessment. Traditional tests and quizzes are given, but ITI teachers also arrange opportunities for students to demonstrate their mastery before appropriate audiences, such as the city council, younger students, or the community at large. This allows students to expand their learning experience by giving them an opportunity to take social or political action by lobbying for their viewpoint, or performing a community service project that requires a range of new knowledge and skills.

Evidence of Results: A statewide program in Indiana, called CLASS, based on the ITI model and implemented by ITI-trained educators, was the subject of several studies. One of the studies analyzed the performance of over 100 CLASS elementary schools on the statewide test. The CLASS schools scored higher than other elementary schools in the state and the scores also increased over time. A second study of 32 students who attended a pilot CLASS school for five years found that the state test scores of this group was approximately one standard deviation above the mean in reading, language arts, and math. A third study on CLASS schools reported that a majority of teachers believed CLASS was having a positive impact on student motivation

and performance, especially on higher-order thinking.

A doctoral dissertation in 1998 compared Texas Assessment of Academic Skills (TAAS) reading scores of students in an ITI elementary school with a control elementary school. Within a two-year period, ITI students' scores showed a 16 percent growth compared to 3 percent growth at the control school. Other elementary schools in Texas showed a pattern of increasing student achievement through TAAS scores after the implementation of ITI.

Compatibility with Service-Learning: The model scored itself as *highly compatible* with service-learning. ITI encourages multi-age, self-contained structures that minimize pull-outs (removing a student from class to attend special instruction) at the elementary level. At secondary levels, teams and block schedules are utilized. Study trips away from school are a consistent feature of ITI. Curriculum begins with in-depth study of nearby locations and ends with social action, often a service-learning project. The ITI curriculum often addresses community needs and this forms the basis for an integrated curriculum component.

Beyond social action as a demonstration of mastery, classroom management is based on the model's *Lifelong Guidelines* and *LIFESKILLS*. According to developer Susan Kovalik, "Positive attitude and acceptable social skills are the foundation for meaningful service learning. In an ITI environment the Lifelong Guidelines and the LIFESKILLS are the preliminary steps before engaging with the community."

Lifelong Guidelines are:

1. Trustworthiness: To act in a manner that makes one worthy of confidence

2. Truthfulness: To act with personal responsibility and mental accountability

3. Active Listening: To listen with attention and intention

4. No Put-Downs: To never use words, actions

and/or body language that degrade, humiliate, or dishonor others

5. Personal Best: To do one's best given the circumstances and available resources

LIFESKILLS are:

- INTEGRITY: To act according to what's right and wrong

- INITIATIVE: To do something because it needs to be done

- FLEXIBILITY: The ability to alter plans when necessary

- PERSEVERANCE: To keep at it

- ORGANIZATION: To work in an orderly way

- SENSE OF HUMOR: To laugh and be playful without hurting others

- EFFORT: To do your best

- COMMON SENSE: To think it through

- PROBLEM SOLVING: To seek solutions

- RESPONSIBILITY: To do what's right

- PATIENCE: To wait calmly

- FRIENDSHIP: To make and keep a friend through mutual trust and caring

- CURIOSITY: To investigate and seek understanding

- COOPERATION: To work together toward a common goal (purpose)

- CARING: To show/feel concern

- COURAGE: To act according to one's beliefs

- PRIDE: Satisfaction from doing your personal best

- RESOURCEFULNESS: To respond to challenges in creative ways

Students help write their own inquiries (learning activities) and can choose which teacher-written ones to pursue. "We recommend a variety of approaches based on Gardner's multiple intelligence's and the highest levels of Bloom's Taxonomy," writes Kovalik. [Bloom's Taxonomy is a tool for categorizing the level of abstraction of questions that commonly occur in educational settings.] Projects can be year-long or short term to provide practice that leads to long-term memory and demonstrations of mastery.

The model features experiential learning methods with "real audiences" and encourages assessments that match the learning goal and student strengths. Processing the experiences of the day via journal writing and cooperative groups called "Learning Clubs" is an important learning strategy and one way for students to reflect on learning activities.

Sources:
Integrated Thematic Instruction, Home Page http://www.kovalik.com/index.html.

McGeehan, J. (2001). *Brain-Compatible Learning*. Retrieved 2002, from http://www.kovalik.com/jmarticle.shtml.

Northwest Regional Educational Laboratory (2001). *The catalog of school reform models*. Retrieved 2002, from http://www.nwrel.org/scpd/catalog/index.shtml.

Women of NASA (1998, April 23). Profiles women of the world. Meet the inspirational women of NASA. Retrieved 2002, from http://quest.arc.nasa.gov/women/TODTWD98/kovalik.bio.html.

LEAGUE OF PROFESSIONAL SCHOOLS

University of Georgia
124 Aderhold Hall, Athens, GA 30602, 706-542-2516, 706-542-2502 fax
http://www.coe.uga.efu.lps

Score: Highly Compatible

"There are extremely competent teachers throughout Georgia, but very few have been equipped to teach in a school where everyone is swimming in the same direction. They are prepared to teach in their own classrooms, but not to help determine as a community what it actually means to be a school." *– Carl Glickman, League of Professional Schools*

Features:

♦ Broad-based school reform effort.

♦ Governing framework to lead schools towards systemic restructuring and a more democratic learning community.

♦ Teachers participate in informed decision-making.

Background: Carl Glickman of the University of Georgia and colleagues created the model in 1990.

Premise: School is a place to prepare students to become productive citizens in our democracy. Successful school change efforts that lead to greater student learning do not happen by simply changing the organizational structure of a school. It comes when the hearts and minds of people in the school, including parents and the community, work together, in a democratic manner, to decide what happens in the classrooms, school's policies, and procedures.

Design: The model's design is focused on a broad-based school reform effort, intending to influence the teaching and learning process. The model does not prescribe a ready-made curriculum, pedagogy, or set of instructional practices. It does offer a framework that establishes a school governing structure to create a democratic learning community to enhance student learning and the effects of these changes on student learning. The design requires a high degree of collegiality among teachers and administrators to initiate substantial changes in classroom practices. The school model's purpose is to impact on how teachers teach, students learn, and parents participate in their children's learning.

The League's school restructuring efforts is based on three guiding principles:

1. Charter: The governance of the school is democratized.

2. Covenant: The focus of the governance is driven by the school's own shared vision of exemplary teaching and learning.

3. Action Research: A "Critical Study Process" is conducted to inform the governance process.

The model believes that this framework will lead a school to create inclusive procedures for gathering and reflecting on information for problem identification, problem solving, and acting collectively. School leadership will move from a hierarchical decision-making system to a democratic process for most decisions made in the school. This change brings a great deal of empowerment to teachers, students, and parents. The League believes, "Democracy is predicated on philosophical and psychological assumptions about humans; specifically, that every individual is an active, curious learner who–given information, materials, and directions–will be able to utilize learning in meaningful ways: to see connections, to discover applications, and to participate with others."

Schools who are looking into the League's model send a delegation or school team made up of staff members, parents, and district personnel to a two-day orientation workshop. The workshop explains the framework of shared governance and action research, focused on curricular and instructional issues. Prospective schools hear from veteran League schools.

As a member of the League, a school can expect to receive:

- four days of central and regional meetings for training and staff planning on the League's framework;

- a biannual newsletter and school directory;

- access to an information retrieval system and network that takes school requests for information about issues, concerns, and practices dealing with the League framework;

- annual site visit by a League staff member or practitioner (other visits can be arranged);

- summer institutes to provide school teams time for team building, analyzing qualitative data, conflict resolution, and grant writing; and

- consultation and technical assistance from League professional staff via telephone, fax, and email.

According to League director, Lew Allen, and League founder, Carl Glickman, it is important that schools take time to decide whether a design is well aligned with where they want to go with restructuring, and understand that substantive changes do not come quickly or easily. The belief system of a school's staff is a strong predictor of their willingness to become a League school. Research done by League staff on participants who joined revealed that a "school's willingness to embrace decision-making and action research was tied to whether its current decision-making process already valued professional reflection, was open to change, recognized teachers as having expertise, and reflected some basic knowledge of the role

that democratic values should play in school renewal." A survey of schools who joined the League revealed characteristics of schools that were more likely to join, such as "a collegial atmosphere where formal and informal discussions about instruction take place; a principal who encourages risk taking, buffets the school from outside mandates, and encourages teacher input in decisions; and faculty members who are informed about and understand the basic purpose for attending the Orientation and Planning meeting.

The League promotes continuous inquiry and improvement in the daily life of schools. Teachers are encouraged to plan collaboratively and are supported by principals who will participate in and facilitate that development. A League school knows that restructuring is a long-term plan that will require substantial time, dedication, and other resources.

Evidence of Results: The Council for School Performance published their independent evaluation on the League of Professional Schools model in 1997. They found that schools that used the model showed increased teacher professional development that led to higher student achievement and a higher number of teachers participated in school governance. Third and fifth graders from League schools scored consistently higher in ITBS (Iowa Test of Basic Skills) and CBA (curriculum-based assessment) reading and math scores, and science and social study scores, against schools without the model.

The study indicates a "need to establish more school reform networks of public schools that are voluntary and ongoing, coordinated and facilitated by universities and other educational agencies, to connect schools that share a similar philosophy, purpose, and commitment to change." Another implication from the study is that school improvements have come through the democratic participation of all members of the school "across roles and grade levels—and not from state mandates and directives."

Compatibility with Service-Learning: The model scored itself as *highly compatible*. The League is now deepening its work from using democratic principles as a guide for school governance to a guide for classroom practices. The League's recent work with "Democratic Learning" has a key premise and belief that student learning should be linked to real issues in their community. Service-learning would thrive well and support such an environment.

The premise of the model and their mission statement are both highly compatible with the ideals of service-learning. The model is working to establish a school environment that promotes the school as a "learning community that is democratic, professional, and student-oriented." Service-learning would thrive well and be supported by such an environment. Both students and teachers are encouraged to take more of an active role in decision making about what is done in the school.

Other highlights of compatibility with service-learning are found in the model. Schools in the League surveyed reported that their students participate in many project activities, and that there is a focus on increasing the quality of student projects at academic fairs. "Parents and community leaders serve and participate in decision-making regarding teaching and learning," and "Our parent and community component provides many activities that our parents participate in." In regard to how civic skills and competencies are addressed, schools responded, "Teachers model shared decision-making with students that will transfer life skills for students," and "Student focused learning along with character education curriculum encourages civic skills."

Schools revealed teaching materials used beyond textbooks, including "accelerated leader, math manipulatives, Learnstar, calculators, computers, laser disks, SRA reading kits, and trade books." One school wrote, "We have been able to provide new materials and programs as a result of our CSR program." Alternative teaching strategies were listed by schools as math labs, reading labs, literacy across the curriculum, peer tutoring, teach story mapping techniques, utilize learning centers, cooperative learning activities, and project-based learning. Interdisciplinary team teaching is demonstrated and encouraged, and portfolios are mandatory. "Teachers are urged to attend and conduct presentations on other assessments," wrote one school. Another wrote, "We are presently exploring portfolio assessment to go along with what we are doing now."

In regards to reflection, schools reported that students are encouraged to write in journals on a daily basis and student-centered instruction includes reflection.

Sources:

Allen, L., Rogers, D., Hensley, F., Glanton, M., & Livingston, M. (1999). *A guide to renewing your school: Lessons from the League of Professional Schools*. San Francisco, CA: Jossey-Bass Publishers.

Allen, L. & Glickman, C. (1998). *Restructuring and renewal: Capturing the power of democracy*. International Handbook of Educational Change, 505-528. Great Britain: Kluwer Academic Publishers.

Appalachian Regional Educational Laboratory (AEL). Comprehensive School Reform Program Catalog. Retrieved 2002, from http://www.ael.org/rel/csr/catalog/leagueprosch.htm

Harkreader, S., Henry, G. T., et al (1997). *Long standing reform effort improves schools: An independent evaluation of the League of Professional Schools*. Atlanta, GA: Council for School Performance, University of Georgia. Retrieved from Council for School Performance http://www.arc.gsu.edu/csp/DownLoad/League.PDF

U. S. Department of Education (1998). The League of Professional Schools in Georgia. In Promising practices: New ways to improve teacher quality. Chapter 6: Improving professional development practices. Retrieved 2002, from http://www.ed.gov/pubs/PromPractice/chapter6.html

THE LEARNING NETWORK®

Richard C. Owen Publishers, Inc.
P.O. Box 585, Katonah, NY 10536, 800-262-0787, 914-232-3977 fax
http://www.rcowen.com

★ ★ ★ ★

Score: Compatible*

"We believe that students become enthusiastic, independent, life-long learners, and accomplished readers and writers when supported and guided by skillful teachers."
– *Richard C. Owen Publishers, Inc.*

Features:

♦ Long-term plan for helping schools organize for effective teaching and learning, using the *Teaching and Learning Cycle*.

♦ Process for working with school leadership, faculty, and community, the *Critical Triangle*.

♦ Professional development, publications, and a network that supports changes in attitudes, understandings, and behaviors of teachers that result in improved learning outcomes for children and long-lasting changes in the way a school organizes for teaching and learning.

♦ Emphasis on building teacher understanding and professional development rather than prescribed instructional materials and lessons.

Background: The Learning Network (TLN) was inspired by conversations that came out of the Literacy Learning in the Classroom summer institute established by the Richard C. Owen Publishers in 1989. Institute participants, educators from the United States and New Zealand, were frustrated by the limited time to explore a cohesive theory of literacy learning. This frustration sparked the idea to create the Network. In 1992, the Richard C. Owen Publishers created TLN to support schoolwide implementation of the Literacy Learning model.

Premise: TLN provides a literacy learning design to support changes in the attitudes, understandings, and behaviors of teachers that lead to improved learning outcomes for children, and long-lasting

changes in the way the school organizes for teaching and learning.

Design: TLN is based on four key principals:

1. Administrators become active and involved instructional leaders, ensuring responsibility and accountability for achieving educational success.

2. Teachers develop a deep understanding of the theory that drives good classroom practice, and become more productive and effective decision-makers.

3. Students thrive in an environment that is consistent from classroom to classroom, grade level to grade level.

4. Schools become learning organizations that are constantly developing and enriching the environment for all members of the community.

A key to the model's design is an instructional process called the *Teaching and Learning Cycle*. There are four elements that "cycle up" in progressive spirals: assessment, evaluation, planning, and teaching. The cycle begins when the teacher takes an assessment sample, such as a writing sample, evaluates the student's knowledge and then plans what to teach next. Careful planning of future lessons builds a scaffold to lift the student to a higher level of understanding. Starting with assessment, the teacher collects data, and with evaluation, she/he plans and then teaches the next learning step. The teacher plans to teach by selecting an objective, grouping the learners, choosing a resource, and determining an approach. The act of teaching finishes the cycle by providing appropriate support in order for new learning to occur. This method of teaching and learning comes from the theory and practice of literacy education in New Zealand. The New Zealand approach was influenced by the research of education philosophers such as John Dewey, Lev Vygostky, Marie Clay, and others.

The model seeks to facilitate reform at the individual, classroom, school, and district levels and has created a management process called the *Critical Triangle* to lead the change process and help restructure the culture within the school. Players in the Critical Triangle include a key administrator (usually the principal), a Learning Network coordinator, and site-based teacher leaders. The Critical Triangle works with the faculty to develop a schoolwide focus and write policies that define the values and objectives of the school. Periodic review and evaluation of the school's policy objectives help to guide future professional development.

TLN has two more features to the design. Instructional dialogue is a professional conversation between a teacher leader and a classroom teacher based upon an observation of classroom practice framed by the teacher's action plan. The goal of the instructional dialogue is to produce new learning for the teacher that will impact classroom practice. Policy statements are documents that connect beliefs of the staff to state and district requirements on reading, writing, spelling, and handwriting. Policy statements provide an active process that helps the school align its collective belief system and culture with the district and state policies and initiatives.

The Learning Network coordinator comes to the school once a month and, with support from the principal, works with the teacher leaders as they begin to work on changes in classroom practice. The coordinator uses instructional dialogue, or professional conversation, to guide teacher leaders through an exploration of teaching and learning designed to result in changes in classroom practice. During the second year,

teacher leaders share this training with colleagues. In the third and subsequent years, TLN training expands to include more of the faculty and to focus on developing the school as a learning organization.

Evidence of Results: Three schools that use The Learning Network model have recently been named as CSR "Promising Sites" by the United States Department of Education. Schools designated as "Promising Sites," according to the model, understand how to identify, gather, and evaluate school-wide data to inform the decisions they make.

The Madison Elementary School District #38 in Phoenix, Arizona began formal involvement with TLN in 1995 and has continued to use TLN as an integral component of the district's literacy component and professional development. In 1998, 1999, and 2000, the students of the district, grades 2-8, scored consistently higher than their peers in county, state, and national averages.

*Compatibility with Service-Learning: The model scored itself as *compatible* with service-learning, however, from their survey responses and an analysis of the model, only marginal support for service-learning could be found. The model does encourage block scheduling at least for reading and writing, and leaves the content and resources used up to the individual teacher and school. This is helpful if the teacher wishes to build a service-learning-driven unit of study that supports reading and writing skills. Within the literacy block, teachers work with children using a variety of resources and experiences, leading to learning outcomes that extend competencies and skills. Flexibility in this area allows input from students and could offer opportunities for service-learning activities or projects. The curriculum content of the literacy block is determined by the teacher and the school, so it would be up to the educator and support from the school culture to provide opportunities to address community needs.

According to the model, "The content of the curriculum reflects the needs and interests of the learner as determined by the teacher, the school, and the community. The instructional resources are selected by the teacher to meet the needs of the individual student." This does not speak to providing opportunities for service-learning to come into the classroom.

According to The Learning Network schools surveyed, students apply academic skills to real-life situations as they participate in oral presentations and peer mediation training. "Civic responsibilities are an ingrained part of our curriculum and daily activities," wrote one school. The model agrees that introduction of civic skills or competencies are left up to individual schools and are not directly addressed by the design.

The model's design supports the idea of reflection, especially during the professional development process. In the description of the model, the developer writes, "Personal and professional growth occurs when the teacher or administrator engages in the reflective process." This may set up educators to model the reflection process to students.

The model's focus lies in developing skillful teachers who make the best instructional decisions based on the evaluation of meaningful assessment data. Team teaching, multi-disciplinary teaching assignments, and multi-age grouping are acceptable within TLN. Project-based learning is not curtailed by the literacy learning model. Teachers rely on a variety of assessments on which they base their evaluation and decisions regarding instruction. A classroom run by a Learning Network teacher is described by the model as "not rigidly organized, or quiet like a library." Instead, students can be seen heavily involved in learning where activity, communication, writing, speaking, movement between and among groups of other students is encouraged.

Sources:

Northwest Regional Educational Laboratory (2001). *The catalog of school reform models*. Retrieved 2002, from http://www.nwrel.org/scpd/catalog/index.shtml.

Richard C. Owen Publishers, Inc. (1999). *Understanding The Learning Network*, Third edition. Katonah, NY: Author.

Richard C. Owen Publishers, Inc. (2001). *The Learning Network: Research and data supporting the content and structure of the Learning Network*. Katonah, NY.

MicroSociety®

13 South 3rd Street, Suite 500, Philadelphia, PA 19106, 215-922-4006, 215-922-3303 fax
http://www.microsociety.org

★ ★ ★ ★ ★

Score: Highly Compatible

"Micro provides a way to implement all the standards. By installing this new operating system, our students are reaching the expectations required by the standards on a daily basis.
– *Triana Olivas, principal, El Paso, TX*

Features:

♦ Developing responsible citizens through community service.

♦ Implementing district and state standards.

♦ Test score improvement strategies.

♦ Making math connections in the real world.

♦ Reading and writing across the curriculum.

♦ Engaging students in experiential learning.

♦ Filling the K-8 gap in career education.

♦ Technology applications across the curriculum.

♦ Building parent participation in a school-wide program.

♦ Developing a school-wide program of community partnerships.

♦ Student service-learning from 'Micro' to 'Macro' Society.

Background: The design was created in 1967 by George Richmond who reasoned that if grades and discipline did not motivate students to learn, perhaps freedom and responsibility would. With this premise, he designed a micro society where basic skills would be relevant to students in their daily lives. The MicroSociety program was first used schoolwide in a Lowell, Massachusetts, K-8 school in 1981. MICROSOCIETY, Inc. (MSI), a national nonprofit organization and home for the design, was founded in 1991.

Premise: Creating a society in miniature in a school can help motivate students, improve basic skills and discipline, achieve high standards, and boost test scores and attendance.

Design: The MicroSociety program motivates students to learn, develop, understand, and apply academic and real-world skills as citizens in a society of their own design. It provides a context for academic learning, builds on the special needs, unique character and resources of a particular school and community, and places special emphasis on the arts, technology, and environmental action and community development. MicroSociety frames learning opportunities around real issues to bring a sense of urgency and relevance to students for acquiring skills to accomplish a specific goal.

The model is integrated into the regular curriculum and is easily tailored to local and state standards. English, math and science curricula comes alive for students when they apply concepts learned to real situations. The intrinsic and extrinsic rewards build self-esteem and motivation in groups of students who are at risk of failing in traditional academic settings.

The design consists of six major strands:

1. Technology
2. Economy
3. Academy
4. Citizenship & Government
5. Humanities and the Arts
6. Heart–Service and Ethics

Twelve essential elements are addressed and combined to make the classroom microsociety run smoothly:

1. Agreement on a Common Purpose

2. Definition of personal goals by teachers and students

3. An internal currency used by students for the operation of their micro society

4. Labor, capital, and information markets

5. Private/public property

6. Organizations such as ventures, agencies, and nonprofits

7. Meaningful contacts with parents and community partners

8. Academics

9. The six major strands listed earlier

10. Teacher planning time for integrating the program with curriculum

11. Jobs and marketable skills

12. Use of real world measures

MicroSociety applies "real learning theory" to students' lives, creating authentic (real) situations that prepare them for the tasks that will face them in their adult lives. The design includes a reading program that guides students to create an entire industry of businesses and services. Math is raised to the level of a survival skill as students become aware that they need arithmetic to buy and sell, create budgets, maintain a checkbook, and deal with other transactions that occur during "Micro" time each day. Students find that they need geometry skills to measure floor plans or design jewelry, and algebra and statistics skills to produce financial reports and spreadsheets. Students take on the role, within the classroom, of architects and engineers to design and build storefronts, test their entrepreneurial skills while using technology to invent or manufacture products for the marketplace. Student government researchers apply biology to recycling campaigns, healthcare

policies and public spaces. Students learn academic skills as they solve problems and serve as resources for each other.

Students are allowed to make the rules that govern behavior in their micro society, and are encouraged to develop internal self-control. As primary stakeholders in ventures and organizations, they play an active role in maintaining order and solving community problems, and they discover the benefit of a secure, cooperative environment where all can flourish. In their micro society, students can create a legislature, make laws, develop a court system that administers them, and launch a group of students, called Crime-Stoppers, who enforce the laws. The Northwest Regional Educational Laboratory summarized, "Because children are deeply involved in rule making and law enforcement, and want to avoid the expense and notoriety of litigation, disciplinary infractions decline. In MicroSociety schools, the peer group allies itself with law abiding interests rather than with outlaws."

MicroSociety is welcoming to parents, community leaders and members. Volunteer roles are important and varied. Parents help by sharing their real world experience with students and teachers.

The model offers teachers professional development and practical strategies for implementing state and district standards. MicroSociety's strategies support a results-driven environment by helping students demonstrate academic and problem-solving skills and by providing schools with a framework for integrating multiple programs into one unified system. Teachers find many opportunities to help students apply academic skills across several disciplines. Student ventures are developed with standards in mind. Even business development strategy is based on standards.

Evidence of Results: According to the Northwest Regional Educational Laboratory, in 1998, an independent evaluator, D. M. Kutzik from Drexel University, examined the impact of the program by looking at nationally-norm referenced tests. The evaluator looked at scores for elementary and middle schools to see the difference between scores for students before and after implementation of the MicroSociety model in the school. Results revealed that after the MicroSociety model was implemented, students showed a 25 percent increase in math over baseline performance, 11 percent increase in language arts, and a 7 percent increase in reading.

Since implementation of the design at the Sageland Elementary School from 1993 to 1998, scores rose on the Texas Statewide Assessment by 216 percent in reading, 178 percent in math, and 22 percent in writing.

In an elementary school in Detroit, Michigan, William Davison School, average 4th-grade MAT (Metropolitan Achievement Test) scores for 1997-98 rose by 43 percent in math, 53 percent in reading, and 24 percent in science.

In Philadelphia's Wilson Middle School, MicroSociety is credited with reducing the number of students scoring Below Basic on the SAT 9 by 10 percent, meeting the districts goals a year early.

A survey of MicroSociety principals nationwide, reported improved attendance and reduced disciplinary infractions after the design was implemented. The model contends that because students are learning by doing, they retain what they have learned longer. Experiencing with direct exposure to experiences and a broad spectrum of careers, they appreciate the skills of visiting adults and the real-life choices that must be made.

Compatibility with Service-Learning: MSI scored its model as *highly compatible* with service-learning. It isn't difficult to see where service-learning lives in this model.

Schools using the model schedule blocks of time for students to tend to their micro "ventures" and agencies, and this may be a substantial commitment of up to three to five times a week.

Schools described the program as allowing students to create a microsociety by applying for jobs, paying rent, taxes and tuition with pay they earn. This society provides a means for students to apply what they are learning to situations of real-life value to them, and of service to others. The service students provide requires them to reach out to the community for information. According to schools surveyed, civic skills and competencies are addressed when students become involved in parts of their micro society that consist of legislature, enforcement, and court. "In addition, students performed community service." "Civic core values—develop civic skills and competencies through seven character traits," wrote one school. Schools described the model design as allowing students to participate in the planning of curricular activities in the following areas: student assemblies, Market Days, legislative meetings, applying for jobs, and starting businesses in the micro society. Textbooks are not used exclusively, according to schools surveyed. Teachers create lesson plans with consultation from professional police officers, bankers, judges, and others who are also invited to present informative workshops for the students. In addition, an extensive amount of curriculum and instructional resources is available from MSI. Through project-based learning, students create products they can sell using student-created currency. Teachers are provided with common planning days to allow them to research, plan together and develop curriculum. "Students use journals, pre and post tests, surveys; they also create news broadcasts, advertisements, and commercials," wrote one school. Students also create rubrics for their products. Reflection occurs in the form of journal entries and class discussion.

A major focus of MSI schools is to involve the local community in the school. The involvement comes from the community members working with the children in their jobs and also the children supporting the community through their nonprofit and service activities.

The sixth strand of the model design, *HEART, service and ethics*, allows teachers to help students build an understanding of their part in the larger community and encourages them to be of service and engage in activities such as fundraising, and outreach. Through the citizenship strand, children gain experience as they participate in the running and governing of their school.

According to the model's survey response, in more advanced MicroSociety schools, the administration merely facilitates. Students write business plans for ventures which guide their experiences in school. The model developer says, "MSI schools increase student's knowledge base well beyond the teacher and the textbook. Children participate in learning by doing, hands-on management of their ventures and agencies." For example, the school currency becomes an effective math tool. Peer tutoring is encouraged, learning by doing is part of the design, and teachers are facilitators.

Projects are long-term and wide-ranging. "For example, students who are successful business owners will manage another business through the school year. Court cases facilitate lawyers' work with defendants, juries, judges, and witnesses to successfully try a case."

One of the major benefits of MSI is cross-grade interaction both for students and teachers. Older children teach younger ones how to read, how to fill out deposit slips and how to argue court cases. Teachers work together to reinforce this learning method in the classroom.

In a MicroSociety school there are multiple ways to succeed as students are assessed through their venture and agency time. Teachers are provided with a number of ways to evaluate progress in real time for every student. "Every child has a job and earns academic rewards as well as regular salaries," wrote the developer. " A child could be a judge, a lawyer, a crime stopper, a business owner, or a bank teller." Students learn to budget money, write resumes and interview for jobs, solve disputes with their peers, and govern themselves.

Through the strong community partnerships, schools can offer students increased outside activities. For example, bank employees visit a bank to learn about its policies and procedures and then apply this to their bank in the micro society."

Reflection is used in the MicroSociety design. Some schools schedule a period for reflection every five or six days. Others use writing and journals to reflect on their experiences. In the classroom, students discuss and reflect with teachers and peers how their experiences relate to the academics they are learning.

Sources:

MicroSociety Home Page http://www.microsociety.org.

Kutzik, D. M. (1998). *MicroSociety program impact on standardized test performance.* Unpublished study, Drexel University, Philadelphia.

Northwest Regional Educational Laboratory (2001). *The catalog of school reform models.* Retrieved 2002, from http://www.nwrel.org/scpd/catalog/index.shtml.

MicroSociety, Inc. (ND). *MicroSociety: An elementary and middle school program,* Information Packet. Philadelphia, PA.

MicroSociety LiveWire Newsletter (Winter 2001). Volume 4, Issue 3.

MODERN RED SCHOOLHOUSE

208 23rd Ave. North, Nashville, TN 37203, 888-275-6774, 615-320-5366 fax

http://www.mrsh.org/

Score: Compatible

"The primary goal of the Modern Red Schoolhouse design is to take the rigorous curriculum, values and democratic principles commonly associated with 'the little red schoolhouse' and combine them with the latest advancements in teaching and learning, supported by modern technology."
– *Modern Red School House Institute*

Features:

♦ Comprehensive design for 21st century schools.

♦ School-based research used to establish needs and priorities.

♦ Teachers trained to design effective instruction aligned to their state standards.

♦ Principals and teachers establish a task force leadership structure.

♦ Technology used to improve communication and enhance instruction.

Background: In 1991, the Hudson Institute in Indianapolis, Indiana was awarded a contract from the New American Schools to develop a design for 21st century schools known as the Modern Red Schoolhouse (MRSH). In 1997, model developers established a nonprofit organization in Nashville, Tennessee to provide technical assistance and support to schools wishing to adopt the design.

Premise: All students can learn and attain high standards in core academic subjects. Students do, however, vary in the time they need to learn and the ways they learn best.

Design: MRSH is a process-oriented design that can be customized to enhance a school's strengths and help schools where they are weak. It helps schools develop high-quality standards-based instruction, performance-based assessments, strong parent and community relations, and organizational practices that support academic rigor and high academic standards. The design can train school staff to: design standards-driven instruction, establish effective organizational practices, implement new technology to manage instruction, expand meaningful learning, and develop parent and community involvement programs that support teachers and students in reaching high academic standards.

The Institute has developed a series of 30 professional development modules for various stages of MRSH implementation. The modules are grouped into main categories that can be mixed and matched depending on the level of implementation chosen by the school and the current strengths and needs of the school. The modules are clustered as follows:

• *Preparing for Comprehensive Change*: Modules in this unit help staff prepare for the types of changes, frustrations, and rewards they can expect as they implement a comprehensive reform design. Here, staff explore the typical stages in organizational change, acquire an understanding of the implications of standards for school organization, classroom instruction, and learning environments. School-based research on student performance and instruction allow teachers and building administrators to understand the strengths on which they can build and the challenges they must address to improve student mastery of their state standards.

- *Setting Sound Practices in Place*: These modules focus on using data instructionally, improving classroom management practices, learning environments, school discipline, character education, and principal leadership.

- *Organizing Your School*: This group of modules supports the school staff in adapting to a task force structure–helping them to improve their use of resources, problem-solving abilities, and "commitment to overcoming obstacles to higher student achievement." All school staff are involved in the development of an effective organizational governance process. Staff choose from six task force areas, such as technology, standards and assessment, curriculum, organization, professional development, and parent and community involvement, and are trained in the relevant scope of work.

- *Building Standards-Based Instruction and Assessment*: This group of modules supports teachers in constructing effective instruction in a standards-based environment.

- *Continuous Improvemen:* These modules conclude the training and focus on ways to insure that students have opportunities for continuous improvement–through differentiated instruction, flexible scheduling, customized plans that address specific responsibilities of the student, the parent, and the teacher–and on ways to ensure that the school has the capacity to continuously improve its ability to serve students through data-driven analysis of problems. The model gives a lot of attention to school organization and participating schools are asked to make a commitment to review their organizational policies and practices to ensure that they are not creating or maintaining barriers to student learning. The model assists schools in devising appropriate responses to their students' needs such as providing some students with more time to learn without holding back others, increasing planning time for teachers, and securing more autonomy and flexibility in the day-to-day operation of the school.

Three important aspects of implementation for the MRSH design are technology, character education, and critical benchmarks.

For technology implementation, schools are asked to bring data, voice, and video systems into the school and install a network and teacher workstations to serve as the backbone of the technology infrastructure. Implementation of technology is spread over three years. The model expects that schools, by the end of the first year, ensure that teachers have access to a word processing system that can support curriculum development. Additional technology can be phased in each year as budgets permit. For example, additional computers can be connected to the network, telephones added to classrooms, and video programming can be expanded. During the implementation period, schools are encouraged to acquire and install a computer for each teacher and administrator with Internet access, CD-ROM, instructional software, and voice mail for telephones and other items. Schools are asked to begin to add supportive computer software and ensure that all school staff can, at a minimum, electronically manage information concerning student progress, utilize the internal and external communication systems, and provide enhanced instruction and learning.

MRSH encourages school staff to be trained beyond the basics of how to use a computer and how to manipulate an electronic portfolio. Students may be asked to assist with trouble shooting along with an in-house expert who is available to all teachers. Teachers are encouraged to use simple technology when developing their instruction. In the second phase of technology implementation, individual student needs are addressed and an instructional management system should be in place.

Character education is an aspect of the design that prepares students for responsible citizenship and employment. Here the model focuses on the development of "habits of action" that include courage, self-discipline, prudence, and a commitment to justice and liberty. The design calls for a conscious effort to encourage virtuous behavior, self-discipline, and honesty. "In the Modern Red Schoolhouse, parents, teachers, and—where appropriate—students are encouraged to identify those values that are most important to their community and, therefore, should be nourished by all those who are a part of school life." The model's underpinning belief is that every aspect of the curriculum and school environment can serve in some way to encourage character development. Community service activities are seen as a way to encourage the development of character, especially responsible behavior and empathy. Also, the model encourages reading and reflection as a way to help students develop appreciation and build character.

Critical benchmarks are formed around six core elements divided into three phases. The core elements are: standards and assessment, curriculum, organization, technology, community involvement, and professional development. The community involvement benchmark is:

Phase 1: Recruit local experts to help with curriculum development;

Phase 2: Establish mentoring system, start pre-school consortium, begin social service support; and

Phase 3: Recruit community volunteers to assist in assessment activities.

Evidence of Results: A 2001 study by RAND Corporation looked at seven CSR models, in school districts located in six states. The MRSH schools in the study were located in the highest poverty areas among the seven designs. Nevertheless, the MRSH model was reported by RAND as most likely to foster gains on state assessments in reading and mathematics. Seventy-three percent of the MRSH schools showed gains in reading that were greater than the district gains and 64 percent of the MRSH schools showed such gains in math.

In 1999, the San Antonio Independent School District research staff conducted an analysis of CSR model effects on school pass rates on the Texas Assessment of Academic Skills (TAAS) for that year. Taking into account the baseline scores of schools, pass rates at MRSH schools were higher than all the comparison groups, which included design team comparisons, as well as schools not partnering with any design team.

The Jackson Public Schools' Department of Planning and Evaluation in Mississippi completed a two-year study of CSR implementation in their district. Baseline achievement data were collected in the district in the fall of 1998 and in the spring of 2000. Researchers compared average gains between the two test periods for schools implementing a CSR design, or model and those with no design. Students at MRSH schools showed significantly higher scores in reading, language arts, and mathematics in the third and fifth grades than students at schools implementing other designs, as well as those not implementing any design.

A longitudinal study completed by staff at the University of Memphis' Center for Research in Educational Policy compared MRSH's only elementary school in Memphis against all other Title I schools in the district. The MRSH school performance gains were significantly better than the comparison group in mathematics, reading, and writing. When the school began implementation of the MRSH design, 28 percent of the 4th graders passed the writing exam. Four years later, 98 percent of the students passed the exam.

In 2001, an independent survey by researchers at the University of Chicago and Tennessee State University found that 70 percent of teachers at third year MRSH sites, and 93 percent at fifth year sites, reported that the model had a significant impact on achievement levels for all students.

Compatibility with Service-Learning: The model scored itself as *compatible*, but there are many areas of high compatibility. MRSH schools often use block scheduling, looping, extended day, and other ways to manipulate time to best serve students. MRSH provides extensive training for teachers in creating performance-based assessments and rubrics to go with the curriculum, and this is quite compatible with service-learning. One school surveyed reported that, "Teachers are encouraged to design curricula which can, does, and could include real-life problems, especially in math."

According to the model, MRSH curriculum training requires teachers to first examine adopted standards and complete inventories that match curriculum and student achievements to standards. Textbooks come into the instructional process later as they are applicable. Schools surveyed revealed flexibility in this area: "MRSH encourages use of outside materials to include trade books, Internet, and community resources," and "If you can dream it, you can do it," wrote one school.

The model provides examples of alternative teaching strategies such as project-based learning, cooperative activities, manipulation, and technology-based learning. "Project-based learning is among the variety of strategies we present to teachers," wrote the developer. Schools revealed that small group instruction, less teacher directed lessons, and more independent and individualized task oriented teaching were being introduced into the classroom.

MRSH schools produce scope and sequences that present all grades and subjects on an interdisciplinary matrix tool. Using this tool, teachers identify appropriate opportunities for interdisciplinary and multi-age teaching. One school wrote, "We had to learn to write interdisciplinary lessons."

The model provides training in alternative assessments, including portfolio assessment and student led conferences, and most units created by teachers trained by the model are encouraged to include reflection as a part of the lesson plan.

Sources:
Modern Red Schoolhouse, Home Page www.mrsh.org.

New American High Schools Development Corporation (1997). *Working towards excellence: Results from schools implementing New American Schools designs.* Arlington, VA: New American High School.

The Modern Red Schoolhouse (2001). *Comprehensive school reform: Research results for Modern Red Schoolhouse. Summary report of independent evaluations.* Department of Planning and Evaluation, Jackson Public Schools, Jackson, Mississippi; Rand, Washington, DC; and Department of Evaluation and Testing, San Antonio Independent School District: San Antonio, TX.

Modern Red Schoolhouse (2001). *The Modern Red Schoolhouse Design: Information Packet.* Nashville, TN: Modern Red Schoolhouse Institute.

ONWARD TO EXCELLENCE II

Northwest Regional Education Laboratory (NWREL)
101 S. Main, Suite 500, Portland, OR 97204, 503-275-9615, 503-275-9621 fax
http://www.nwrel.org/scpd/ote

Score: Neutral

"To succeed in an improvement effort and induce long-term systemic change, research shows it takes a quick start, the involvement of a whole community, and initial results within a year. And it takes on-going support to sustain improvements over time." – *Robert E. Blum, developer*

Features:

♦ School leadership teams

♦ School profiles, data on student achievement

♦ Two-year, 10-step improvement process

♦ Effective-practices research supports design

Background: Onward to Excellence (OTE) was developed in the early 1980s at the Northwest Regional Educational Laboratory. The design has been updated to incorporate new knowledge. The name has been changed to reflect the revision.

Premise: To build the capacity of education and community organizations to engage in long-term systemic change efforts aimed at improving the performance of children, youth, and young adults.

Design: The OTE II design involves an approach that, according to the developer, "helps school communities work together to set goals for student achievement, use research and data to drive decision making, and build capacity for continuous improvement." A School Leadership Team and an External Team are created. The School Leadership Team, including the principal, staff members, community members, and sometimes students, leads the school faculty through the improvement process. The External Study Team collects data and monitors school improvement. A facilitator, or Coach, is selected to guide the school improvement process.

The OTE II approach to school reform involves every individual in the school system–from students and school faculty, to the superintendent and board members, to parents and other community members. This brings all stakeholders together to establish a common purpose related to student learning and to work toward fostering a sense of community.

The design approach of OTE II is to guide school communities towards accomplishing seven system outcomes.

1. Ensure quality and equality in the learning of all students.

2. Reach agreement about and secure commitment to a mission and student learning goals.

3. Ensure that what students learn, how they learn, and how they are assessed aligns with the mission and goals.

4. Ensure that the mission and goals drive human, financial, and other resource decisions.

5. Involve stakeholders who represent the diverse roles, perspectives, and cultural composition of the community whenever planning and making improvements.

6. Collect and study data to improve decision making throughout the improvement process.

7. Create and sustain a 'learning organization' that uses its own experience and knowledge and that of others in carrying out its work.

The model's process to help schools reach the outcomes consists of four interrelated phases:

1. *Setting Direction*

2. *Planning Action*

3. *Taking Action*

4. *Maintaining Momentum*

Components in the process Setting Direction, for example, include setting a common purpose, mission and vision, stakeholders working together to improve learning for all, setting common standards for student learning, and establishing agreed upon school improvement goals. Activities in each phase are continuous and the progress and insight acquired through each provides information for the work to move forward in subsequent phases. For example, in the Planning Action phase, educators learn to make professional decisions about practice. Their experiences during this phase help them make more informed decisions in the Taking Action phase. "The processes are interrelated and iterative. Plans are made, action is taken, reflection occurs, and plans are updated. The process continues in this manner," wrote the model developer.

Evidence of Results: *An Educator's Guide to Schoolwide Reform* from the American Institutes for Research found the design had a marginal rating of success on affecting student achievement.

There is some research that shows student performance does improve when the model is properly implemented. The model reports that schools and districts in Oregon, Washington, Mississippi, and Alaska have provided evidence that achievement scores and other student outcomes improve when OTE II is implemented with strong school and district leadership. Two studies conducted by NWREL on schools in the northwestern states and Mississippi demonstrate that OTE II leads to greater teacher collaboration and research-based teacher practices in schools, and that when the process is faithfully implemented OTE II schools show larger student achievement gains than non-OTE II schools.

Compatibility with Service-Learning: The model developer's combined score from the survey was *neutral*, but on some questions the scores were compatible. Also, some questions were left un-scored or commented on by the developer.

The possibility of block scheduling is left up to schools to consider as they work to incorporate effective practice. The model does not support or defend the idea of providing opportunities for students to apply their knowledge and skills to real-life situations, problems, or projects. "This depends on decisions made by the school as they work to improve practice," wrote the model developer. The model does not address local community needs in its design and does not, for example, support the idea of students as volunteers. Decisions regarding the development of civic skills and competencies are left up to the schools. The use of alternative teaching strategies is, again, up to the school and teacher. Project-based learning may be used if schools decide this is an effective way to achieve their improvement goals. Interdisciplinary team teaching and/or experiential learning methods may be used if this is chosen by the schools as something to include as part of the design of their curriculum. The use of alternative assessments and reflection is also a decision for the school to make.

Sources:
Onward to Excellence II, Home Page http://www.nwrel.org/scpd/ote/description.shtml.

American Institutes for Research (1999). *An educators' guide to schoolwide reform*. Retrieved 2002, from http://www.aasa.org/issues_and_insights/district_organization/Reform/overview.htm.

Northwest Regional Educational Laboratory (2001). Onward to Excellence: Carrying the Flame. Portland, OR.

Onward to Excellence (June 15, 2000). Onward to Excellence: Information Packet. Portland, OR.

PAIDEIA

University of North Carolina, School of Education
P.O. Box 26171, Greensboro, NC 27402, 336-334- 3729, 336-334-3739 fax
http://www.paideia.org

Score: Highly Compatible

"All learning is active, not passive. It involves the use of the mind, not just the memory."
– Mortimer Adler

Features:

♦ Measures each child's progress individually

♦ Includes three instructional techniques and professional development for teaching and learning:
  • Didactic (lecture) instruction
  • One-on-one coaching
  • Socratic seminars

Background: The Paideia model is based on a manifesto published in 1982 by Mortimer Adler. Adler and his colleagues developed twelve Paideia principals and proposed a relationship between three types of teaching: didactic instruction, coaching of intellectual skills, and seminar discussion. Through a partnership between Adler and University President William Friday, the National Paideia Center was established at the University of North Carolina in 1988. Terry Roberts is the current director of the Paideia Center. Ted Sizer, developer of the Coalition of Essential Schools, was an original member of the Paideia Group.

Premise: High academic achievement is expected of all students. A high quality education is essential to democracy.

Design: The Paideia model was greatly influenced by philosopher and educator, Mortimer Adler, a man steeped in classical education, harking back to Greek literature. The term Paideia is loosely translated from the Greek language to mean "the upbringing of children." These influences are seen in the essential elements of a Paideia classroom. A Paideia classroom is a student-centered classroom dedicated to the learning of all students. In the classroom, assessment of students and teachers is individualized rather than standardized in order to emphasize individual growth. The classroom is dedicated to the intellectual development of both children and adults, and fits into a larger school community dedicated to lifelong learning.

The Paideia approach is an attempt, as Teacher Magazine writer, David Ruenzel writes, "to infuse public schooling with a new intellectual vitality." In the same article, a principal in Charlotte, North Carolina described the type of teacher that works well with the Paideia program. "In order to teach in a Paideia environment, you have to be a person of real intelligence–a kind of Renaissance person. You need to know something about everything. This doesn't mean you'll know all the answers– indeed, that's not the point of Paideia–but you have to know how to ask the right questions."

The Paideia model is based upon 12 principles summarized as follows.

1. All children can learn.

2. They deserve the same quality of schooling, not just the same quantity.

3. The quality of schooling to which they are entitled is aligned with what parents want.

4. Schooling at its best is preparation for becoming generally well educated, and schools should be judged on how well they provide this preparation.

5. Schools should prepare all Americans for three callings: to earn a decent livelihood, to be a good citizen of the nation and of the world, and to make a good life.

6. The primary cause of genuine learning is the activity of the learner's own mind, sometimes with the teacher functioning as a secondary cause.

7. Three types of teaching should occur in school: didactic teaching of subject matter, coaching that produces the skills of learning, and Socratic questioning in seminar discussion.

8. The results of the three types of teaching should be: the acquisition of organized knowledge, the formation of habits of skill in language and math, and the growth of the mind's understanding of basic ideas and issues.

9. Each student's achievement of these results would be evaluated in terms of their own competencies and not related to the achievement of other students.

10. The principal of the school should not be an administrator only, but should be a leading teacher who should be cooperatively engaged with the school's teaching staff in planning, reforming, and reorganizing the school as an educational community.

11. The principal and faculty of a school should themselves be actively engaged in learning.

12. The desire to continue their own learning should be the prime motivation of those who dedicate their lives to the profession of teaching.

The Paideia plan has a formula of balance among didactic, coaching, and seminar processes. The developer believes that in a well-planned unit of study, a teacher's didactic presentation should not exceed 10-15 percent of class time. Coaching, or a Coached Project is student work time where facilitation of discussion can come from the teacher, or by students for students, and should occur 60-80 percent of the time in a classroom. Finally, the Padeia Seminar should occupy 15-20 percent of class time.

The Paideia program requires teachers to reconfigure the school year into a series of Coached Projects. In this setting, teachers coach students in academic skills as they work together through a project. A Coached Project is similar to a traditional unit of study in that it is generally two to three weeks in length. It involves several disciplines and engages multiple intelligences and a context for practicing different intellectual skills. The Paideia model sees the Coached Project as a rehearsal and practice that precedes a recital or presentation. According to the model, students are very much involved in the planning and assessment of progress toward a product of real-world value. The Coached Project often has an audience in the world outside the classroom, so students become vested in producing a quality product. As described in the Paideia program, "It is what gives the entire project—and the academic work it contains—relevance for the students doing the work."

Authentic, student-centered assessment is found in all three areas of the Paideia method of teaching and learning. As the model's ninth principle of learning states: "Each student's achievement of these results would be evaluated in terms of that student's competencies and not solely related to the achievement of other students." According to Terry Roberts, director of the National Paideia Center, Paideia teachers "do not equate intellectual quality with standardized test scores. Rather, they measure each child's progress individually and communicate about that progress as clearly and helpfully as possible."

Assessment in the Paideia classroom is done as a cyclical process that involves teachers and students. Together, teachers and students identify their curriculum goals, diagnose their status relative to those goals, plan strategies to achieve those goals, measure progress along the way, and evaluate where they are in relation to meeting their goals. In the Coached Projects and Paideia seminars, assessments such as rubrics and checklists are used to evaluate the level of achievement or success of a project or discussion.

Paideia's Professional Development program falls into three phases plus an evaluation in which teachers, administrators, and parents in the school community receive instruction and guidance:

- Phase 1: Seminar leadership, and seminar discussion for a consistent schoolwide instructional technique. Paideia staff provide both the training and technical assistance during the school year and assist the principal in establishing a schoolwide implementation plan.

- Phase 2: Planning and Implementing Coached Projects. Didactic instruction and coaching academic skills through "product-oriented" student projects are addressed. Teachers, with assistance from parents and administrators, plan a series of Coached Projects for students to work independently and in teams to produce high quality work. Teachers integrate seminar instruction into each unit of study to build on the knowledge and skills acquired through didactic and coached instruction.

- Phase 3: Training in assessment and curriculum. Here, assessment and curriculum planning skills necessary to complement and support seminar teaching and academic coaching are addressed.

- Evaluation Plan: The evaluation plan involves evaluation assistance, evaluating the process of implementation, and identifying and evaluating the major outcomes on schools, community, parents, teachers, and students. Here, participants learn to assess and describe the degree and nature of implementation of the Paideia program and assess the effects of this implementation on the school, community, teachers, parents, and students.

Evidence of Results: Former Guilford County, North Carolina, superintendent Jerry D. Weast reported in an October 1997 article to the American Association of School Administrators:

> Another staff development approach that has shown great promise came through collaboration with the National Paideia Center. The training has helped our teachers acquire instructional methods that emphasize skills that the business community seeks in employees. Our students are learning to think, reason, organize their thoughts and respect the opinions of others.

A four-year study of Paideia implementation in Guilford County North Carolina, commissioned by the School Board of Guilford County and conducted by the Center for Educational Research and Evaluation at the University of North Carolina, Greensboro, revealed descriptive results about Paideia implementation across grade levels and subject areas. Examples of results are as follows.

- Teachers at all Paideia sites reported that students improved their critical thinking and ability to express themselves clearly.

- The achievement effects in schools committed to Paideia increased at a faster rate than in other schools.

- Implementation of Paideia was associated with classes with reduced friction: "...students are calm and not mean, and students feel safe."

- The implementation of Paideia had positive effects on students' self-concept of ability, achievement, family self-concept, and confidence in self.

- Fully implementing Paideia can reduce the negative effects of social comparison.

Compatibility with Service-Learning: The model scored itself as *highly compatible* with service-learning. The Paideia program and service-learning are similar in many respects. Although service-learning is not overtly mentioned by the model, it is evidenced in examples of Coached Projects. For example, one teacher turned a problem at school into a Coached Project. When a six-foot high, red clay bank, separating the playground from the back of the school began to erode and creep progressively closer to the school after each rain storm, students were challenged to develop a solution. Students studied erosion in a water table built in the classroom. The class was divided into five design teams. Each team developed a model and method to stabilize the bank to prevent further erosion and solve the problem. Students drew their ideas, wrote detailed descriptions and explanations as to why they thought their designs would work. A 25-foot segment of the bank was divided into five sections and each group spent many days during recess working with parent volunteers to apply their tested method to stabilize a section of the bank. Two-weeks later, after their methods were tested by a hard rainstorm, students and teachers evaluated each group's method for containing the bank. Issues of cost and time to execute each method were discussed. The class decided on the best solution to stop the erosion and the school's maintenance team agreed to use it to fix the entire bank. Students asked to finish the work together on a Saturday without help from the school's maintenance crew. Coached Projects and Paideia seminars lead students to take on real-world problems where academic skills are learned as they imagine a solution, develop a method, and solve the problem.

Other elements of service-learning are seen within the model. Flexible use of time such as block scheduling is used by the model. "Although we do not require flexible use or time, seminar practice requires longer periods of academic time, so that we recommend floating the schedule to fit instruction."

There are options for students to apply their knowledge and skills to real-life situations, problems, and projects. "All Paideia Coached Projects are designed to access real-life audiences by producing products of authentic value outside the classroom," wrote Terry Roberts, executive director. One school

surveyed wrote, "In Paideia, 60 percent or more of student work should be project oriented."

The model addresses local community needs whenever possible through Coached Projects. "Coached Projects are intended to address real-life community issues and problems in order to make the curriculum relevant," noted one school surveyed.

The model's curriculum includes objectives for developing civic skills and competencies. "Our seminar practice develops interpersonal social skills and our Coached Projects are often community-based," wrote Roberts. The model allows students to play a role in planning curricular activities. "They are supposed to help design the Coached Projects and then assess progress all along the way."

The model allows teachers to use a variety of learning materials other than textbooks. "We may use a wide variety of seminar 'texts' and real-world materials as part of our Coached Projects," wrote one school. Teachers are free to use any materials as long as they are accountable to district standards," wrote another.

The Paideia approach allows teachers to use alternative teaching strategies. "We not only allow, we require creative use of the Paideia Seminar and Coached Project," wrote Roberts. The model's instructional methods include project-based learning. "The Paideia Coached Project (our unit-design model) is based entirely on product-oriented projects. It is one of our mainstays," wrote one school.

The model's approach to curriculum allows teachers to use interdisciplinary team teaching and/or experiential learning. "We strongly encourage the use of interdisciplinary Coached Projects all the way through senior high school," wrote Roberts. Alternative assessments are allowed or encouraged. "In both Paideia Seminars and Coached Project, we require teachers and students to use checklists, rubrics, and portfolio assessments."

The model allows or provides time for student reflection. "Our seminars require reflection both during and after seminar dialogue–as a standard part of the strategy," wrote Roberts. According to one school, with Coached Projects and group time, student interaction is a must.

Sources:

National Paideia Center (2001). *Paideia Active Learning*, University of North Carolina, Greensboro, NC.

Northwest Regional Educational Laboratory (2001). *The catalog of school reform models*. Retrieved 2002, from http://www.nwrel.org/scpd/catalog/index.shtml.

Roberts, T. (1999). *The Paideia classroom: Teaching for understanding*. Greensboro, NC: The National Paideia Center, University of North Carolina.

Ruenzel, D. (1997, May/June). Look who's talking. *Teacher Magazine*, 26-31.

University of Auckland, School of Education, New Zealand. Paideia . Retrieved 2002, from http://www.arts.auckland.ac.nz/edu/staff/jhattie/Paideia.html.

Weast, J. D. (1997). *When bigger can be better*. American Association of School Administrators. Retrieved 2002, from http://www.aasa.org/publications/sa/1997_10/weast.htm.

QuESt™

Educational Concepts
4 Office Park Circle, Ste. 315, Birmingham, AL 35223, 205-879- 9160, 205-879- 9161 fax
http://www.qes-quest.com

★ ★ ★ ★

Score: Compatible

"Quality is necessary for public education to thrive in the future. We have a moral imperative to use quality to make a difference in the lives of children." – Diane Rivers

---

Features:

♦ "A3" implementation cycle: Assess, Align and Achieve.

♦ Total Quality Management principles are applied to schools and districts, based on Malcolm Baldrige criteria for quality in education.

♦ Curriculum alignment and instructional mapping.

♦ Standards-based process.

♦ Full audit at school level to include all stakeholders, including parents, students, teachers, and administrative staff, before developer begins restructuring process.

Background: Quality Educational Systems– Tools for Transformation (QuESt) was developed by Diane Rivers, president and founder of Quality Educational Systems, Inc. (QES) in 1989. Rivers is an experienced educator with over 30 years of experience as a classroom teacher, educational psychologist, building and system administrator.

Premise: Improvement occurs at the process level; therefore, to improve schools, processes must first be addressed. When multiple processes in the school are improved in a holistic manner, significant progressive school change can occur quickly.

Design: QuESt is a comprehensive continuous improvement model designed to create and sustain high-performing, quality schools. It works in partnership with K-12 institutions to link quality principles to systemic practices. QuESt is implemented in three phases: auditing, planning, and development. The A3–Assess, Align, Achieve implementation cycle is a hallmark of the QuESt model. The model seeks to improve student achievement by aligning schools' processes with best practices and strategic plans.

In the first phase, the model developer conducts a Quality Educational Audit that will enable the school and district to see its strengths and weaknesses. Establishing a baseline for strategic improvement, the audit identifies a process for the transformation of the school to begin. In the second phase, QES introduces Strategic Quality Planning and Design to help schools identify their mission and vision, align educational practices with sound educational philosophy and research, identify processes to drive the school's performance, infuse quality principles and practices into the school's process, and develop a set of integrated strategies to ensure the school's vision. In the third phase, the model's Quality Development and Deployment program is introduced to provide comprehensive training and professional development for school staff.

The QuESt model is guided by seven quality principles.

1. Mission-Driven Schools.
2. Total Quality Leadership.
3. Customer Focus.
4. Continuous Improvement of Processes.
5. Data-Driven Decision Making.
6. Continuous Learning Environments.
7. Team Leadership and Team Membership.

There are ten key process areas used by QuESt schools to assess performance: philosophy, mission, organizational structure, curriculum, instructional strategies, assessment, professional development, interdisciplinary teaching, team structure, and community collaborations.

Evidence of Results: In 1994, Wilkerson Middle School, a QuESt school in Birmingham, Alabama, received the prestigious USA Today/ Rochester Institute of Technology Quality Cup. According to the model, a number of QuESt schools have received recognition from their state's Quality Award Program (based on the Baldrige criteria).

Compatibility with Service-Learning: The model scored itself as *compatible* with service-learning. Many service-learning features can be found within the model's design. The model allows for flexible use of time, e.g., block scheduling. According to Diane Rivers, "QuESt assesses schools' use of flexible scheduling and supports organizational changes to provide flex time for learning cycles." Flexible use of time is important to allow students to become engaged in a service-learning project that requires them to visit the community.

The model provides opportunities for students to apply their knowledge and skills, to real-life situations, problems, or projects. "QuESt assesses and supports the use of alternative assessment and team based project learning through professional development," wrote the developer.

The QuESt curriculum addresses local community needs. "QuESt assists schools in conducting consumer satisfaction surveys and interviews to identify community needs and work with community collaboration teams," wrote Rivers. The curriculum includes objectives for developing civic skills and competencies. "QuESt assists schools in mapping and implementing state standards, including social studies standards and objectives that address civic issues," wrote Rivers. The model allows students to play a role in planning curricular activities, and encourages teachers to gather input and use student interest and ideas to design interdisciplinary units.

The QuESt design is flexible and allows teachers to use a variety of learning materials other than textbooks, encouraging teachers to use standards to guide curriculum. Alternative teaching strategies such as interdisciplinary team teaching are used, and teachers are encouraged to develop grade level projects and teach groups of students in cooperative learning settings. Instructional methods include project-based learning.

Alternative assessments are allowed or encouraged. "QuESt encourages the use of a variety of alternative assessments, including projects, presentations, and provides professional development to build skills and knowledge," wrote Rivers. The model allows or provides time for student reflection in journal entries, and classroom dialog and discussion. "QuESt assesses and supports the planning of lessons that include student reflection, classroom discussion and self-evaluation as an instructional process."

Sources:
QuESt, Home Page http://www.qes-quest.com.

Advancing Performance Excellence (January 2000). *Quality progress: Twenty-one voices for the 21st Century*. Milwaukee, WI: American Society for Quality.

Northwest Regional Educational Laboratory (2001). *The catalog of school reform models*. Retrieved 2002, from http://www.nwrel.org/scpd/catalog/index.shtml.

QuESt Quality Educational Systems(2001). Toolkit for a Quality Fit.

Roots and Wings (Success for All)

200 West Towsontown Boulevard, Baltimore, MD 21204-5200, 800-548- 4998, 410-324- 4444 fax
http://www.successforall.net

Score: Somewhat Compatible

"We want our children to have roots–the academic foundation, self-concept, and positive attitude on which success in school depends. We want our children to have wings–the thinking skills, creativity, flexibility, enthusiasm, and broad world view to soar beyond the commonplace."
– *Robert Slavin and Nancy A. Madden*

Features:

♦ Early intervention for preschoolers

♦ Reading program emphasizing systematic phonics

♦ Writing/language arts program

♦ Math program

♦ Integrated social studies and science program

♦ School-family support team for home-school collaboration

♦ One-to-one tutoring for children

♦ Professional development, implementation checks, and follow-up training

Background: Roots and Wings was created in 1992 by Robert Slavin and Nancy A. Madden of The Johns Hopkins University and the Success for All Foundation. With a grant from the New American Schools Development Corporation, they extended their reform approach into the main areas of the elementary curriculum not addressed by Success for All. (Created in 1987, Success for All is a widely-used whole-school reform model focusing on reading, writing, and language arts in the elementary grades.) Roots and Wings subsumes Success for All. The Success for All and Roots and Wings programs combined to form the new Success for All Foundation on July 1, 1998.

Premise: Every student should receive a firm foundation in the knowledge and skills needed to succeed in today's world.

Design:The New American School's *Blueprints for School Success: A Guide to New American Schools Designs* describes the basis of Roots and Wings as having Roots, or strategies, to ensure that every child can meet world-class standards: early intervention for preschoolers, research-based curriculum with extensive training support, one-to-one tutoring for children struggling with reading, and family support. Wings refers to improvements in curriculum and instruction designed to let children soar.

As an extension to the Success for All school design, Roots and Wings combines five areas, reading, writing/language arts, math, science, and social studies through programs designed to meet the educational needs of children in grades 1-6. Programs include: *WritingWings*, an approach to writing that emphasizes the use of peer response; *MathWings*, a constructivist-based mathematics program; *WorldLab*, a project-oriented curriculum using simulations of real-world events to integrate social studies, reading, writing, science, fine arts, and other areas; individual tutoring by paraprofessionals, teachers and volunteers; a full-time facilitator; family support; and professional development and training for teachers.

Components of Roots and Wings are implemented into the school over a three-year period. In the first year, schools phase in components of Success for All's reading program. These components are: The Early Learning Program, Reading Roots and Reading

Wings. *WritingWings* is introduced, emphasizing the use of four-member peer response groups where students help each other plan, draft, revise, edit, and publish their work. Language arts instruction is integrated into the writing lessons.

In the second year of implementation, *MathWings* is introduced. *MathWings* is a mathematics program based on the standards of the National Council of Teachers of Mathematics. Students learn mathematical concepts through construction of knowledge, development of problem-solving processes, and discovery through exploration. *MathWings* utilizes assessments such as performance tasks, observations, concept checks, journal writing, problem-solving, and interviews with students to make instructional decisions and to evaluate each student's growth.

Worldlab is introduced to the school in the third year of implementation. It provides a curriculum that integrates social studies and science curriculum for grades 1-6. As described by the developer, *Worldlab* is a laboratory where students can utilize and enhance the skills they are learning in other components of the Roots and Wings program, including reading, writing, and mathematics." It allows students to form cooperative groups to learn about the world through simulation exercises and by investigating real-world problems and issues.

Worldlab takes a thematic approach to learning and provides units of study for each grade-level. Themes for units may include: Trees, Harvest, Birds, Changes, Forests, Harvests Around the World, Life Cycles, Africa, Japan, Archaeology, Germ Hunters, and others. Teachers follow the Roots and Wings outline to move through lesson plans. Teachers "Set the Stage" for students to review key concepts about a topic, provide "Active Instruction," incorporating techniques such as "Thinking Out Loud," modeling and demonstrations; encourage "Teamwork" among students to complete investigations, experiments or simulations; and they provide "Time for Reflection" to discuss and defend ideas and to reach consensus. Finally, teachers introduce a concept called *Extend and Connect*, to get students to apply the concepts learned to other situations. *WorldLab* is the Roots and Wings program most compatible with service-learning.

Key elements must be in place to begin a successful implementation of the Roots and Wings design. A full-time facilitator provides assistance to teachers. Tutoring is provided to first graders who have serious reading difficulty. A family support team provides support to parents in ensuring the success of their children. There is a commitment among school staff to reduce the number of special education referrals and retentions. A Building Advisory Committee is established to provide assistance in shaping program policy and to guide development of policy. Scheduling adjustments are made to accommodate 90-minute blocks of time for reading and *Worldlab*, 60-minutes for math, and no less than nine tutoring sessions per tutor. Schools and classroom libraries may need to be supplemented with more material to support the *WorldLab* curricula.

Evidence of Results: Before the implementation of Roots and Wings, students in four high-poverty schools in rural St. Mary's County, Maryland performed below the state average on the Maryland School Performance Assessment Program (MSPAP). In 1993-96, evaluations of the model found strong positive effects on the MSPAP. Roots and Wings students gained significantly more than students in the state as a whole on all six MSPAP scales in third and fifth grades and also exceeded state averages.

The state of Tennessee carried out an independent evaluation of Roots and Wings and found similar results on the Tennessee Comprehensive Assessment Program. They compared 22 high-poverty Roots and Wings schools in Memphis to control schools. Results revealed that before the Roots and Wings program was introduced the schools performed far below the control group. After four years of implementation of Roots and Wings, the school's scores were substantially higher than those for the control group or other district schools.

Compatibility with Service-Learning: (This section includes quotes from the model developer and schools.) The model scored itself as being *somewhat compatible* with service-learning. Roots and Wings' *Worldlab* component is highly compatible with service-learning because it:

- engages students in the meaningful pursuit of knowledge;

- promotes an understanding of the interdependence of economic, political, biological, and physical systems;

- uses simulation, group investigation, experimentation, and cooperative learning;

- guides students in completing products that help solve community problems;

- encourages problem solving and higher-order thinking processes; and

- involves community members as a resource for students.

"*Worldlab* certainly emphasizes experiential learning methods, and interdisciplinary teaching. It always includes science, social studies, and writing," writes Robert Slavin.

The model allows for flexible use of time, such as block scheduling. "Homerooms make for easy flexibility. In middle school pilots, we work towards block scheduling with varying degrees of success," wrote one school.

Roots and Wings students apply their knowledge and skills to real-life situations, problems, or projects, "often with simulation, and sometimes in actual projects in the community in schools working with the *Worldlab* component," writes Slavin.

Community needs are addressed. The family support team interacts with the families and community agencies to address family needs and connected community needs.

Teachers use a variety of learning materials other than textbooks, particularly in *Worldlab*, such as: the Internet, interviewing, and speeches. Alternative teaching strategies such as cooperative learning and simulation are core strategies in the model's design. Project-based learning is used in *Worldlab* as are alternative assessments. The model provides opportunity for reflection by students, "in every area." Students are encouraged to play a role in planning curricular activities only in the *Worldlab* component.

Sources:

New American Schools (1998). *Blueprints for school success: A guide to New American Schools designs*. Arlington, VA: Educational Research Service.

Ross, S. M., Sanders, W. L., Wang, L. W., & Wright, S. P. (July 2000). Value-added achievement results for three cohorts of Roots and Wings schools in Memphis: 1995-1999 Outcomes. Baltimore, MD: Center for Research on the Education of Students Placed At Risk, Johns Hopkins University.

Ross, S. M., Sanders, W. L., Wright, S. P., Stringfield, S., Wang, L. W., & Alberg, M. (2001). *Two- and three-year achievement results from the Memphis restructuring initiative. Schools effectiveness and school improvement*. Baltimore, MD: Center for Research on the Education of Students Placed At Risk, Johns Hopkins University.

Slavin, R. E., Madden, N. A., & Wasik, B. A. (1996). "Roots & Wings: Universal excellence in elementary education." In S. Stringfield, S. Ross, & L. Smith (Eds.) *Bold plans for educational reform: The New American Schools*. Hillsdale, NJ: Erlbaum.

Slavin, R. E., Madden, N. A., & Wasik, B. A. (1997). *Success for All and Roots & Wings: Summary of research on achievement outcomes*. Baltimore, MD: Center for Research on the Education of Students Placed at Risk, Johns Hopkins University.

Slavin, R. E., & Madden, N. A. (2000).

Roots & Wings: Effects of whole-school reform on student achievement. *Journal of Education for Students Placed At Risk, 5* (1-2), 109-136.

Slavin, R. E., Madden, N. A. (May 1999). *Roots & Wings: Effects of whole-school reform on student achievement* (Report No. 36). Baltimore, MD: Center for Research on the Education of Students Placed At Risk, Johns Hopkins University.

SCHOOL DEVELOPMENT PROGRAM
(THE COMER PROCESS)

Yale University
53 College Street, New Haven, CT 06510, 203-737-1020, 203-737-1023 fax
http://www.schooldevelopmentprogram.org/

Score: Compatible

"Our program promotes development and learning by building supportive bonds that draw together children, parents, and school." – *James P. Comer*

Features:

♦ District-wide reform model involving teachers, parents, school board members, central office staff, and community stakeholders in redesigning urban schools.

♦ Structure as well as a process.

♦ Applying principles of child and youth development.

♦ Literacy process.

♦ Balanced curriculum process to align curriculum with standards and assessments.

Background: The School Development Program (SDP) school model was conceived in the late 1960s by child psychiatrist James P. Comer. He observed children's experiences at home and in school and found that such experiences deeply affect a young person's psychosocial development, which in turn shapes their academic achievement. Comer concluded that a child's poor academic performance is in large part a function of the failure to bridge the social and cultural gaps between home and school. Comer's school design was first implemented in 1968 in two low-achieving schools in New Haven, Connecticut. In an effort to solve the problem of lack of trust and positive interaction among parents, teachers, and administrators, and the need for a structure for change, Comer developed SDP.

Premise: SDP is based on Comer's metaphor of six developmental pathways along which children mature—physical, cognitive,

psychological, language, social, and ethical. The SDP process is based on key assumptions:

• Children come to school with developmental gaps resulting from a lack of developmental support at home, impairing their ability to learn.

• Despite this deficit, society still expects all students to meet high standards dictated by the workplace and civic needs.

• SDP recognizes this problem as an "experience deficit" and does not accept the "academic deficit theory" that leads to lowered expectations and tracking of minority and English-as-a-Second-Language (ESL) students.

• All students can reach high levels of academic achievement and are entitled to high quality education that meets high levels of academic achievement.

• Academic learning rests on six developmental pathways: physical, psychological, language, social, ethical, and cognitive.

• Schools must provide students with rich experiences and opportunities to reach their highest potential.

• Schools cannot do this alone and must mobilize adult stakeholders, particularly parents, to help meet the developmental needs of children.

Design: The model's systemic approach to education reform focuses mainly on school governance, standards, curriculum and instruction, parent involvement, and psychosocial support for staff and parents.

The SDP design is built on a framework in which stakeholders (educators, parents, school staff, and administrators) are organized into three teams that operate under three guiding principles: 1) *no fault*–shifting the focus to problem-solving rather than blame; 2) *consensus decision-making*–decisions made through dialog and understanding and a focus on what is good for children and youth; 3) *collaboration*–the principal and faculty teams work together. The School Planning and Management Team includes administrators, teachers, support staff, and parents, and is responsible for developing a comprehensive school plan, sets academic, social and community relations goals, and coordinates school activities, including staff development programs. The team discusses issues of teaching and learning, monitors progress, supports and makes adjustments to the school plan. The Student and Staff Support Team includes the principal, staff members in child development and mental health, such as counselors, social workers, psychologists, or nurses. The team coordinates student services, individual student needs, resources in the community, and develops prevention programs. The Parent Team is composed of parents, some of whom serve on the School Planning and Management Team. This team develops activities designed to engage parents in supporting the school's social and academic programs.

A component of the SDP design has been added to help schools and districts focus on principles of child and youth development as they relate to curriculum and instruction. The Learning, Teaching, and Development Unit (LT&D) strategies:

- create smooth transitions from home to preschool and school;

- align teaching, learning, and assessment with students' developmental needs and abilities;

- balance the curriculum with content that enhances students' overall development;

- help schools improve the literacy, mathematics, and critical thinking skills of their students so they are prepared to meet local, state, and national standards;

- help schools improve the academic skills and development of all students so they can reach their highest potential;

- enhance the capacity of adults to make more effective decisions about teaching and learning; and

- help schools make the connection between governance and management and classroom practices.

The model's Professional Development and Consultation unit helps schools and districts build support systems needed to fully implement the "Comer Process." SDC professional development includes leadership training through a Principals' Academy and an Academy for Developmentally Centered Education.

Evidence of Results: The American Institutes for Research's, *An Educators' Guide to Schoolwide Reform* lists the SDP as showing "promising evidence of positive effects on student achievement."

According to SDP researchers, the model has a history of evaluation and research conducted by their own staff and outside evaluators. Their research examined school climate, level of program implementation, students' self-concepts and behavior, social competence, and achievement. Where the Comer Process was followed consistently, SDP schools show a significantly greater reduction in absenteeism and suspension when compared to other district schools. Also improved were student self-competence and achievement.

Results from the 1999 Third International Mathematics and Science Benchmarking Study (TIMSS): Guilford County students in Greensboro, North Carolina scored 27 points above the international average in mathematics and 46 points higher than the international average in science. Guilford County eighth graders scored 12 points above the national average in mathematics and 19 points above the national average in science. The dropout rate in Guilford County has fallen to the lowest level among large districts in the state.

Compatibility with Service-Learning: The model scored itself as *compatible* with service-learning.

SDP provides teachers and administrators with an in-depth understanding of child and adolescent development. With this expanded knowledge-base, teachers, parents, administrators, and other staff come together, through the School Planning and Management Team (SPMT) and the Curriculum and Instruction Subcommittee to make decisions regarding scheduling. "The decision comes from within the school," wrote Sherrie Joseph from the office of Executive Director Edward T. Joyner. Therefore, if service-learning is important to a school using the SDP model, it can be incorporated into the school's schedule.

The model's design provides opportunities for students to apply their knowledge and skills to real-life situations, problems, or projects. "The SDP provides teacher training in developmental instructional practices. These practices encourage teachers to structure their classrooms to include more hands-on activities, the application of higher order thinking skills, real-life problem solving, and out of classroom learning opportunities," wrote Ms. Joseph.

The curriculum addresses local community needs. "Through the Student Staff Support Team and Parent Team as well as SPMT, the education stakeholders look at the barriers to learning that students face and in turn develop programs and intervention strategies to eliminate those barriers. Some of those barriers are health and housing," wrote the developer.

The model allows students to play a role in planning curricular activities. In middle and high school, students participate in SPMT. The SPMT is charged with making decisions about the curriculum and instruction. SDP encourages staff to have ongoing dialogue with students about their learning. Feedback from these dialogue sessions is used to modify the curriculum where appropriate.

The SDP model encourages teachers to use a variety of instructional practices that are relevant to the developmental level of the students as well as their interest and learning styles. Through the work of various subcommittees and teams, staff and parents are asked to create opportunities for learning to extend into the home and community. "We also have two programs that encourage creativity in instruction," wrote Joseph. Teachers Helping Teachers is an SDP program designed for teachers to review four highly interactive, non-textbooks-driven teaching models.

Alternative assessments where reflection is addressed are encouraged, through portfolios, teacher-made tests, performance assessment, and journal writing.

Sources:

American Institutes for Research (1999). *An educators' guide to schoolwide reform*. Retrieved 2002, from http://www.aasa.org/issues_and_insights/district_organization/Reform/overview.htm.

Comer, J. P., & Woodruff, D. W. (1996-97). School Development Program. Center for Effective Collaboration and Practice, Yale University. Retrieved 2002, from http://www.air-dc.org/cecp/resources/success/comer.htm.

Northwest Regional Educational Laboratory (2001). *The catalog of school reform models*. Retrieved 2002, from http://www.nwrel.org/scpd/catalog/index.shtml.

School Development Program Model Information Packet (2000).

School Development Program (September 2001). The Comer Process.

TALENT DEVELOPMENT

Johns Hopkins University, Center for Student Placed at Risk (CRESPAR)
3003 North Charles St. Suite 200, Baltimore, MD 21218, 410-516-8800, 410-516-8890 fax
http://www.csos.jhu.edu

Score: Somewhat Compatible

"These are bold schools; it takes courage and commitment to take on such sweeping reforms. But what we're finding is that the staff of these schools have a real hunger to create a safe, serious learning environment in their schools, a place where the success of every student is possible."
– *James McPartland, director of the Talent Development High School, CRESPAR*

Features:

♦ Ninth grade success academy

♦ Four-period day

♦ Common core curriculum

♦ Curriculum and instruction innovations

♦ Career academies

♦ Twilight school

♦ Professional development

Background: The Talent Development model was created in 1994 through a partnership between researchers and practitioners at the Center for Students Placed At Risk (CRESPAR), based at Johns Hopkins University, and Patterson High School, in Baltimore, Maryland. Patterson High School, slated for reconstitution due to poor performance, was the first site to implement the Talent Development model.

Premise: The Talent Development initiative has created a design to address the problem of excessive numbers of youth dropping out during their first year of high school. Talent Development was created to provide students entering high school with learning opportunities, motivation, and supports needed to overcome poor prior preparation and successfully complete a core curriculum.

Design: Talent Development was made for large high schools that face challenging problems with student attendance, discipline, achievement scores, and dropout rates. The initiative is a prescriptive school model that focuses on providing students with learning opportunities, motivation, and support needed to successfully complete a core college prep curriculum. The model features an organization and management plan, data collection of school climate and student achievement, curriculum and instruction innovations, and parent and community involvement to encourage preparation for college and careers. A basic set of college preparatory academic courses is required of all students.

Talent Development's design elements include:

• Block schedule, 80-90 minute classes to keep students engaged in class longer and out of trouble in the hallways.

• Introduction of a common core of college preparatory curriculum for ninth grade students with emphasis on extra time for English and mathematics.

• Required courses for students in the ninth grade: "Freshman Seminar," "Transition to Advanced Mathematics," and "Strategic Reading."

• Intensive and subject-specific professional development for faculty and curriculum coaches for ongoing classroom-based implementation support.

• Self-contained career academies for grades

10-12 to provide a core academic curriculum, work-based learning experiences, and career-focused pathway teams of students and teachers.

- Student-centered teaching strategies such as team and cooperative learning during longer period classes.

- Alternative after-hours Twilight School for students with attendance or discipline problems, or for those transitioning to school from incarceration.

- Use of data to provide feedback to teachers and administrators about the impact of the model on student outcomes and school climate.

- An organizational facilitator who works full-time assisting principals and staff with planning, data collection, changes in facilities, and leadership issues.

- Curriculum coaches for on-site professional development and in-class implementation support for teachers.

- Curriculum materials for first-term freshman courses.

The model design offers a *Ninth Grade Success Academy*, a school-within-a-school, to provide a smooth transition for new students entering into the high school experience. CRESPAR believes it is important to physically separate ninth grade students from the rest of the school. This is done by placing the Ninth Grade Success Academy on a separate floor, or in a separate wing of the high school. An assistant principal oversees and has an office within the Academy. Teams of six teachers, led by a team leader, instruct a common group of 150-200 students in an interdisciplinary manner. Teachers are provided common planning time.

The four-period day creates longer class periods that provide more time for individual assistance and enable teachers to get to know their students better. According to the developer, "Extended class periods allow teachers to use instructional strategies such as cooperative learning and projects that engage students' attention." The longer class time also makes it possible to complete a year-long course in one semester, enabling students who have been retained to accelerate. It is also possible for students who have been retained to be promoted to the tenth grade in the middle of the school year. For example, at Strawberry Mansion School in Philadelphia, 63 repeating ninth graders earned enough credits to be promoted to the tenth grade after the first semester.

The ninth grade curriculum offers intensive academic experience "designed to break the cycle of failure which is epidemic in large, urban, non-selective high schools." Every ninth grader in need receives a "double dose" of mathematics and English instruction. A typical ninth grader would have a schedule with Strategic Reading in the first semester, moving to English I in the second semester; Transition to Advanced Mathematics in the first semester, moving to Algebra I or Integrated Mathematics in the second semester; science or elective, moving to science or elective; and Freshman Seminar, moving to social studies or history in the second semester.

Students who need extra help to reach their academic goals are offered a number of chances to get ahead: Summer School, Saturday School, and after-hours Credit School. For troubled students who are found to be unmanageable during regular school hours, have become afraid of school due to issues such as bullying, have life issues that make getting to school in the morning hours impossible, or who are transitioning to school from incarceration, the model has developed Twilight School. Twilight School is an alternative after-hours program that offers instruction within small classes, an inviting learning environment, mentoring, guidance, support staff, and other services. The school is open each afternoon and evening of the week. In addition to earning academic credit, students are offered an opportunity to receive ongoing counseling from the school psychologist or social worker. The Twilight School has its own professional staff including a principal, a lead teacher, three core subject area teachers, Special Education teachers, and counseling staff.

Talent Development offers a professional development component for faculty called *Four Tiers of Teacher Support*. The first Tier includes curriculum-specific professional development. For each course, the model has developed two to three days of summer training, followed by a few hours of monthly professional development. The professional development provides modeling for upcoming lessons, content knowledge, effective instructional strategies, and classroom management techniques. The second Tier of support provides highly trained peer teachers who give weekly in-classroom implementation assistance. Trained lead teachers within the school give the third Tier of support. Instructional facilitators from Johns Hopkins University provide the fourth Tier of professional development.

Evidence of Results: After one year of implementation, Talent Development model researchers interviewed students from a Talent Development school site and compared their answers with responses from students at a control school. This research revealed that use of the model improved students' perceptions of the school climate. Students in the Talent Development School found cutting class to be tougher, hallways quieter, and students roaming hallways less. Sixty-six percent of the Talent Development students found their school to be safe versus 59 percent of students in the control school. Forty-six percent said their school was clean versus 36.5 percent in the control school. The research also revealed that the most striking change in the initial year of implementation was the creation of an orderly climate in the school, decreases in suspensions and arrests, and improvements in attendance. According to the developer, these changes led to better grades. Their research further revealed that the percent of first-time freshmen passing English, Algebra I, and science in 1998-99 and 1999-00 in the Talent Development School was significantly higher than in the control school: 55.8 percent

verses 39.9 percent.

Researchers Dick Corbett and Bruce Wilson interviewed 160 ninth and tenth grade students at two Talent Development high schools in the spring of 2000. Their interviews revealed that students were relieved to discover a calm, friendly environment in place of the hostile and stark school depicted in rumors among their peers. Three quarters of students identified the four-class schedule as a major reason why teachers were able to work closely with them.

An independent researching firm, Research for Action, interviewed ninth grade teachers at two Talent Development high schools. Their interviews revealed that teachers were encouraged by their students' achievement gains, students' use of study skills learned in the Freshman Seminar, assistance of the Curriculum Coaches, and support provided by the Team Leader.

Compatibility with Service-Learning: The model rated itself as *somewhat compatible* with service-learning.

Talent Development's responses to the survey reveal a few areas of strong compatibility with service-learning. Three components of the model's design: a four-period day with blocks of time (80-90 minutes long), interdisciplinary curriculum teams, and career academies for grades 10-12 provide a solid environment for the introduction of service-learning methodology. It may be possible to introduce instruction or activities that allow students to apply what they have learned to projects or products that address real-life issues. The model's career academies do provide shadowing work-site visits and internships. However, the model does not mention if students are encouraged to apply what they have learned to create something of value, something that provides evidence of their skills to an employer, or answers a need within the community. With thoughtful planning, the model could build in expectations for the career academies to encourage students to use the skills they are learning to address a community need. In nursing or health academies, students could visit nursing homes and create a brochure or booklet to explain the effects of aging in an attempt to build intergenerational understanding. In a business academy, students could be encouraged to assist a small community business, or local non-profit. CRESPAR admits on the survey that the model's curriculum, at this time, puts little thought to including community needs or the development of civic skills or competencies, but it does not rule this out. The model also does not allow students to play a role in planning curricular activities. However, the model is "on the way" to developing instructional methods that include project-based learning, bringing alternative assessments such as student portfolios and presentations into greater focus, and providing time for structured student reflection in the form of journals, classroom dialog, and discussion.

Sources:

The Talent Development, Home Page http://www.csos.jhu.edu/Talent/high.htm.

Center for Research on the Education of Students Placed At-Risk (CRESPAR) (2001). *The Talent Development High School: First-year results of the Ninth Grade Success Academy in two Philadelphia schools 1999-2000.* Philadelphia, PA: Philadelphia Education Fund.

Center for Research on the Education of Students Placed At-Risk (CRESPAR) (1999). *The Talent Development High School with career academies.* Baltimore, MD: Johns Hopkins University.

Corbett, H. D., & Wilson, B. L. (2000). *Students' perspectives on the ninth grade academy of the Talent Development High Schools in Philadelphia: 1999-2000.* Philadelphia, PA: Philadelphia Education Fund.

Rice, L. (1999). *Thirty-two schools re-open as Talent Development Schools. Demand for Johns Hopkins' whole school reform models grow.* Headlines@Hopkins. Baltimore, Maryland: Office of News and Information, Johns Hopkins University. Retrieved 2002, from

http://www.jhu.edu/news_info/news/home99/sep99/talent.html.

Walker James, D. (1997). *Some things do make a difference for youth.* Washington, DC: American Youth Policy Forum, 55-57.

VENTURES EDUCATION SYSTEMS CORPORATION

245 5th Ave, Suite 802, New York, NY 10016, 800-947- 6278, 212-696- 5726 fax
http://www.vesc-education.com/

Score: Compatible

"This problem-based learning movement became more organized when a new nonprofit group, Ventures In Education (VIE), was formed to work with the Macy-sponsored high school programs to expand their achievements into other schools nationwide. Macy schools were working on improving the performance of students in science, and VIE wanted to spread such efforts to other schools. VIE also wanted to encourage schools to use problem-based learning in a variety of curriculum areas." – *Maxine Bleich, president, Venture's Education Systems Corporation*

Features:

◆ Student-centered learning.

◆ Interdisciplinary project learning that incorporates problem-based learning.

◆ Professional development programs.

◆ Activity books for teachers and students that align Ventures' instructional strategies with required district and state assessments.

◆ Teaching manuals that align Ventures' instructional strategies with curriculum, lesson plans, standards, and district and state assessments.

◆ Courses for graduate, district, and continuing education credit.

◆ Ventures Scholars Program–Educational and career linkages to college, university, and post-graduate institutions.

Background: The concept of Ventures was born from the Affirmative Action movement of the 1960s to increase minority access into higher education. The Macy's Foundation, creator of Ventures, was deeply involved as a leader in advancing minorities into the medical field. In the 1980s, the Foundation began an initiative to form collaborations between high schools and universities recognizing secondary schools as partially responsible for inadequately preparing students in mathematics and science and other academic studies needed to enter college. In 1990, Ventures In Education, Inc. was formed as a nonprofit corporation by the Macy

Foundation "to prepare economically disadvantaged minority high school students for medicine and other health related professions." In 1993, Ventures received funding from the National Science Foundation for the establishment of a three-year, schoolwide initiative to include administrative restructuring, teacher enhancement, and curricular enrichment. In 1997, the Ventures Education Systems Corporation was launched to provide a vehicle for distribution of proven research-based and applied systems of learning, including the *Ventures Initiative and Focus®* system of student-centered learning and other related products and services.

Premise: Replace teacher-centered learning with student-centered learning. Educators learn how to implement a student-centered approach through the use of constructive communication and the development of literacy and critical thinking skills aligned to the curriculum and local and national standards.

Design: The Ventures design strives to educate schools to provide conditions necessary for the successful implementation of student-centered learning. The model employs a combination of instructional approaches that help students "develop and internalize literacy, analytical reasoning, and problem-solving skills." A special focus is placed on applying "constructive communication and group process in the classroom to get teachers and, ultimately, students to become deeply engaged in student-centered learning." Skills learned through this process can be applied to course content and in students' daily lives. The model developer has designed interdisciplinary projects and problems that are aligned to local, state, and national standards across disciplines and has connected these to the student-centered learning process.

According to the model, constructive communication takes place in an environment that teaches students to work collaboratively in groups, listen attentively, speak coherently, and appreciate thoughts and opinions different from their own.

Educators are taught through Ventures' Professional Development program to build skills in their students by bringing four basic elements into their teaching methodology.

1. A non-stressful environment conducive to human interaction and thinking.

2. The ability to coherently verbalize thinking.

3. An understanding of individual differences that may affect communication.

4. Effective group process.

The Ventures approach to establishing effective student-centered classrooms includes:

- Implementation and integration of student-centered thinking skills necessary for mastery of content.

- Literacy Instruction I: for the early grades, K-3.

- Literacy Instruction II: for the later grades, 4-12.

- Constructive communication, group process, literacy and structured thinking skills applied to content through the vehicle of problem-based learning.

- Student-centered, interdisciplinary project learning.

- Standards alignment.

- Focused strategic planning.

Project-based learning is incorporated with problem-based learning and involves students in what the model calls a "real-life design project," an activity that could easily be mistaken for service-learning. Here, students incorporate the arts, communication skills, core curriculum, and school-to-work initiatives, all aligned with standards, to investigate and problem solve. Teachers use "project statements" based on real situations such as stage productions, the building of a comprehensive high school, or the creation of a waste disposal plant. An interdisciplinary team including a mix of teachers, tradespeople, government officials, and other community members work together with students on the project. Through this project, students develop skills that can be applied in their everyday lives. Projects vary in length from one week, several weeks, a semester, or an entire academic year to complete.

Teachers at Paramount High School, a Ventures site in Alabama, presented students with a community challenge. Students were told that local businessmen in Greene County, Alabama proposed to build a solid waste disposal facility along a stretch of the East Bank of the Tombigbee River and had secured $1.2 million to fund the project. The businessmen wanted a model of the facility to be presented that would represent the positive influence the project could have on the community. A group of high school students, an interdisciplinary team of teachers—science, math, social studies, a school counselor, and a community resource group consisting of environmental protection, earth sciences, design, architecture, engineering, and construction joined to meet the challenge. Students worked on site to document conditions with photographs, maps, and sketches; visiting cultural, historic and architecturally significant sites for reference. Through their problem-solving process, meeting with various professionals, students learned how designers utilize basic core disciplines and practical applications of statistics, geometry, measurements, physics, botany, and chemistry. As a result of their experience, students proposed that an Environmental Education

Center with a small exhibition and learning center be built along with the waste disposal facility. With this addition, waste recycling and landfill engineering could be explained to the public. Although their proposal was not realized, the students were internally motivated toward future higher academic performance from the experience.

Walks of Life, a program under the care of Ventures In Education, Inc., is an example of a community and work-based partnership project between education and industry in New York City. The model developer believes school-to-work skills are a natural part of the learning process, not separate. The *Walks of Life* provides connections between work and school-based activities from kindergarten to the senior year. *Walks of Life* links schools with community-based organizations and assists schools to develop meaningful literacy and work-related service-learning experiences for students. The partnership project also works to help students find summer employment. It offers staff development for educators and industry representatives to help them provide high quality, meaningful school and work-based learning activities. Examples of *Walks of Life* projects are:

- Elementary Schools

    - Junior Achievement, a six-week program taught by university students interested in education, recruited by Walks of Life from local colleges.

    - Classroom presentations and company visits in the private and public sector organizations, from a variety of industries, provide activities that include all subject area classes. Walks of Life arranges for volunteers to meet with classes to discuss the SCANS (Secretary's Commission on Achieving Necessary Skills), education, and experience involved in their jobs and explain how skills learned in class relate to careers.

    - KAPOW is a monthly program where employee volunteers are recruited to partner with schools to teach children about what they do at work. Students visit the volunteers' workplaces and participate in hands-on, work-related activities.

    - Intergenerational program pairs students with continuing care facilities to visit senior citizens twice each month. Students work and participate in history projects, career discussions, arts and craft activities, and reading and writing.

    - World In Motion is a hands-on program that helps students see how engineers use math and science to solve everyday problems.

- Intermediate Schools

    - Classroom presentations, company visits and Career Day.

    - Service-learning programs link schools with a variety of community-based organizations to develop meaningful literacy and work-related service-learning experiences. The program works with youth to help them find summer employment.

- High Schools

    - *Walks of Life* works with school personnel to recruit sites for this after-school community service work and develops evaluation materials for agency coordinators and students. This program is also tied to summer employment opportunities.

    - Career Paths Internship program offers opportunities to high school juniors and seniors to participate in a two-afternoon per week, year-long, unpaid work experience.

    - College preparation activities offer high school seniors college-related workshops, scholarship searches, college shadowing, visits to the Job and Career Center, and development of a portable skills portfolio.

Evidence of Results: Ventures helped seven schools in Louisiana raise eighth grade scores in

English language arts, on the Louisiana Educational Assessment Program for the 21st Century (LEAP 21), a criterion-referenced test (This kind of test is based upon the content all children are expected to learn. Scores are based on the amount of content a student demonstrates compared to a predetermined passing score). Some were raised from eight percent of students reaching the Basic level of achievement in 1999 to 13 percent in 2000. In math, five percent more students scored at the Basic level in 2000 from the previous year. Results of the test also showed a significant drop in students in both fourth and eighth grades scoring at the Unsatisfactory level from 1999 to 2000.

The NWREL online catalog of models reported that a 1990 study by the McKenzie Group (education and business consultants) revealed positive findings on the impact of the Ventures program, including evidence that students scored considerably higher on the SAT than their same-race peers across the country.

Compatibility with Service-Learning: The model scored itself as *compatible* with service-learning. The model makes explicit reference to service-learning in the *Walks of Life* program. It also hinges on project-based and problem-based learning, student-centered learning, and interdisciplinary learning–all elements strongly tied to service-learning.

The Ventures model allows for flexible use of time, an important component to service-learning, and provides professional development for teachers in problem-based learning and project learning.

The model does not provide a curriculum, but relies on the existing curriculum used in the school, so if the school chooses to bring service-learning into the curriculum, it will not interfere with the model design. Also, if the school allows students to play a role in planning curricular activities, the model will not interfere. The Ventures program does not preclude a school from including students in planning curricular activities.

The model allows for the use of alternative learning materials beyond regular textbooks.

The use of alternative teaching strategies is the core of the Ventures model, and project-based learning, a strong component of service-learning, is introduced by the model in the third year of the design. Interdisciplinary teaching and service-learning are at the heart of the model's design. Alternative assessments such as portfolios and presentation ceremonies are used.

The model provides for an optional school-to-career program in high school that includes job shadowing and internships. The model design does provide time for student reflection through journals, and one-on-one discussions.

Sources:

Delisle, R. & Bleich, M. (1997, Fall). Affirmative Action in Medical Education. *NESPA Newsmaker*, 2-10.

Jamar, J. (1997). Architectural youth program builds scholars. *Alabama Arts*, Spring, 16-20.

Northwest Regional Educational Laboratory (2001). *The catalog of school reform models*. Retrieved 2002, from http://www.nwrel.org/scpd/catalog/index.shtml.

Ventures Education Systems Corporation (2000). *Louisiana test scores in seven schools that have worked with VESC for one or more years*. New York, NY: Author.

Ventures Education Systems Corporation Information Packet.

Ventures Education Systems Corporation (2000). *The Ventures Initiative and Focus® system of student-centered learning*. New York, NY: Ventures Education Systems Corporation.

CONCLUSION

Service-learning is a powerful tool for reaching both the academic and social objectives of education. It has the potential to reinvigorate the education reform movement by encouraging the creation of a caring community of students to improve the school's culture and positively impact our world. The formal embrace of service-learning by more school reform models would be a positive step. However, there are barriers to the adoption, implementation, and sustainability of service-learning in more of the nation's schools.

Service-Learning Barriers:

1. Some teachers (and school boards) find it easier to stick with the "three Rs."
2. The service-learning definition needs standardization so that all efforts have the same basic characteristics.
3. Some educators question the willingness of organizations to accept middle-grade students as volunteers, and the issue of supervision of younger students must be addressed.
4. Some teachers complain of a lack of time for planning and time for student participation.
5. Service-learning may be seen by some educators as another initiative to deal with, and in doing so, they may pass it off as an add-on activity.
6. Before implementing service-learning, teachers need training or orientation in planning, implementation, and evaluation.
7. There is a relative scarcity and accessibility of quality placement sites, especially in rural areas where little transportation is available.
8. The cost for a full- or part-time service-learning coordinator is or can be prohibitive.

These issues are not insurmountable and with dialog, careful management, fundraising, and planning can be overcome.

Aligning Service-Learning and Education Reform

Implementation and sustainability of quality service-learning is better facilitated when a school or district aligns it with educational goals and dedicates a professional and permanent staff position to oversee and guide the initiative. The role of school and district leaders in the adoption and implementation stages of service-learning is key. Without an onsite champion, even teachers passionate about service-learning will find it difficult to sustain resources or the environment needed to bring service-learning experiences to life. Support from stakeholders can push service to the forefront of education reform as a recognized, supported, and integral element in the life of a school and its community and ease educators' hesitation toward community involvement. The introduction of service-learning into a small portion of the school's program, where staff can focus on quality and depth of practice, is a good start. Also, a clear understanding among school staff, parents, and students of the delineation between service-learning and regular volunteering activities not linked to academics will reduce confusion.

Bridges can be built to foster alignment between the worlds of service-learning and education reform if leaders in both fields reach out to each other. School models could highlight service-learning in their design and introduce it during training and technical assistance. School reform conferences could extend an invitation to service-learning leaders to be keynote speakers or session leaders. Service-learning conferences could reciprocate. More teachers' colleges could offer courses on creating quality service-learning for all grade levels and in major subject areas. Schools could offer incentives to educators to take the initiative to integrate service-learning into their standards-driven curriculum. School districts could reach out to community leaders for ideas and support, such as classroom visits from business leaders, trade professionals, and innovative scholarships for students who implement service-learning projects that have an exceptional impact on the community.

States could post free online databases of state standards linked to a curriculum building tool that includes an option to integrate service-learning. Sample online listings of quality service-learning, standards-driven curriculum units or lesson plans for each grade level, in English language arts, math, science, history, social studies, and other areas could be amassed and shared as a resource. Policymakers could list service-learning training as an allowable activity for district and school professional development funds. Some states and districts have encouraged their service-learning programs to correlate with school-to-career or workforce skills such as those seen in the broad academic and workplace skills developed by the Secretary's Commission on Achieving Necessary Skills (SCANS). SCANS promotes the idea that students learn best when they are taught in a context of application, or functional context. School-to-career strategies and service-learning have much in common and are linked in local districts such as the School District of Philadelphia and Boston Public Schools, and in states such as California, Minnesota, and Oregon. "Linking service-learning and school-to-work both requires and facilitates strong community partnerships. These partnerships can build strong relationships and often set the stage for comprehensive education reform" (National Association of Partners in Education, 2001, p. 24).

The federal government could expand its Learn and Serve America initiative to give support to more schools and districts wishing to adopt service-learning methodology, or expand service-learning to more students and teachers. The National Service-Learning Leader School program, a peer reviewed competition, could be strengthened and expanded to provide more substantial grant awards to schools competing for the title.

Service-Learning Can Improve Schools and Communities

"A new partner has stepped boldly forward to help shoulder the burden of improving schools and communities. That partner is the young people themselves." – *James C. Kielsmeier*

There are many interesting stories of disengaged students who have come back to education because their interest was sparked through involvement in a service-learning activity, helping them find meaning and purpose in learning. This report will end with two compelling stories of students engaged in service-learning activities.

A group of eighth-graders from the Academy of Science and Foreign Language Middle School in Huntsville, Alabama, was touring the Maple Hill Cemetery. After hearing thorough biographical descriptions of important 19th century citizens of Huntsville who were buried in the cemetery, the students asked if any were African Americans. Their question brought the tour to a halt. The guide could not answer but discovered later that the cemetery for Civil War veterans, former governors, and other upstanding individuals in the community was for "whites only."

Students and teachers of the Academy, a National Youth Leadership Council "Generator School," began a journey to discover where Huntsville's African Americans from the last century were buried. In their journey, students discovered Glenwood Cemetery, a resting place for African Americans, with unmarked graves, vandalized headstones, and poorly kept records. Teachers responded to the students' interest to recover the lost information from Glenwood. With the help of their teachers, students created the Alabama African American History Project as they embarked on their community contributions and learning experiences.

Students led the restoration of Glenwood Cemetery, raising funds to repair or replace up to 166 headstones, and the state responded positively to their request to place an official registry sign at the cemetery. Math classes plotted the previously unmapped site, using resources donated by the University of Alabama. Some students searched court records, city council minutes, family inventories, and The Negro Gazette, a locally published newspaper from the 1800s. Students listened to recorded oral histories looking for information on the people buried in the cemetery. Curricular materials developed by the students from original historical sources are now the basis of a third-grade social studies unit about the history of Huntsville, Alabama. Students asked state legislators to change a state law to preserve Glenwood cemetery. This student-led service-learning project is now tied to the Academy's government classes and is still in progress (Kielsmeier, J.C. , Phi Delta Kappan, May 2000, pp. 654-655).

Rivers Middle School students in Charleston, South Carolina, transformed their neighborhood of rundown properties and began to map the neighborhood and learn more about it. The students asked the mayor and the city council to increase fines and strengthen code enforcement against negligent property owners. They asked a judge hearing these cases to levy the maximum fines allowable by law. As a result of the student interest, the council and the mayor's office created an action plan to improve properties identified by the students. The judge worked with the students to see how the law could be interpreted to pursue out-of-state property owners. These examples show how service-learning can encourage civic engagement (Richardson, S., Generator, p. 20-21).

The students in these stories applied academic skills and learned first hand how the branches of local and state government work to enforce, create, and interpret the law. Service-learning experiences help youth: acquire and use information, become engaged in the world around them, communicate, cooperate, and make judgments. Service-learning is a viable partner and ally those involved in education reform and community renewal.

APPENDIX

The Study

This study reports on the responses from leading CSR programs or models to a survey featuring 12 key elements of service-learning. Originally, 33 models were approached and 28 completed the survey and were included in the study. The intent was to analyze survey responses and ascertain the degree to which each design incorporates the key service-learning components into their curricular and instructional approaches, or general program structure. Selected schools, up to four per CSR model were sent the same 12-question survey. Schools were included in the study in an attempt to provide a practitioners' view. Not all school reform models summaries in this study are accompanied by comments from a schools. Getting surveys back from schools proved very difficult.

It was interesting to visit the worlds of each school model to observe variations on themes in education reform and innovations in school design. Education reform is a large field and staying focused on service-learning elements in light of a kaleidoscope of curriculum developments and education philosophy was challenging. Most models had a general understanding of service-learning, but had not given a lot of thought to integrating the term into their model design. And, many models are using key elements of service-learning while not recognizing it as such.

Survey Method

A wide net was cast, through questions on the survey, to gain an understanding of major school reform models' knowledge and use of service-learning or service-learning-like activities incorporated within their design. Originally, 20 questions based on attributes of service-learning, recognized by the service-learning field, were included on the survey. Before the survey was distributed to models and schools, the list was shortened to 12 questions, reducing the size of the survey and increasing the probability of it being returned. The survey asked CSR models and schools to rank their school reform program's compatibility with the 12 questions. The survey also asked for explanation of the rank, or score, and left room for comments. Survey participants scored their school model design on a 0 to 5 point system.

> 0 for No
> 1 for Do not know, or Not applicable
> 2 for Sort Of
> 3 for On the Way
> 4 for Yes, and
> 5 for Strong Yes

A short definition of service-learning was provided on the survey for those not familiar with the term.

> "One definition of service-learning is community service connected to academics. Service-learning is also described as 'bringing real-world meaning and purpose to classroom projects or assignments,' and 'methodologies that integrate academic and technical skills and applied learning.'"

The data collected for the study are too small for statistical significance and are not extensive enough to allow the study's conclusions to be generalized. However, looking at the results of the study will help build a clearer understanding of leading school reform programs and their degree of compatibility with service-learning.

CSR model developers were asked to return the survey along with an updated information packet describing the school model. School models were also asked to provide a list of schools that had used the model for at least two years. Most models complied, but some were cautious about sending a list. Some school names were acquired from the National Clearinghouse for Comprehensive School Reform, Northwest Regional Education Laboratories, and the school model web sites.

A similar survey and letter was prepared for principals of schools who have implemented the school reform model. The research was focused on finding similarities between the school model design and elements of service-learning, rather than comparing the perception of quality for the program between the models and schools. In several cases, models scored themselves lower on some questions for which the schools scored them higher.

Up to five attempts through mail, fax, and phone were made to obtain completed surveys from both the models and schools. Most surveys came back fully scored and with numerous comments. Very few models scored themselves as "somewhat compatible" or "neutral" with service-learning. This signaled that a notable degree of compatibility between school reform and service-learning early in the study.

As surveys and information packets trickled in, analysis began. A summary of each school model was written to provide information to the reader including the background of the model, premise of the design, design elements, evidence of results, an analysis of compatibility with service-learning and a pertinent descriptive quote on the model.

Survey Questions

The survey questions were developed jointly by Robert Bhaerman and Sarah S. Pearson.

1. *Does the CSR model allow for flexible use of time, e.g., block scheduling? If yes, please explain.*

2. *Within the CSR model, are there opportunities for students to apply their knowledge and skills, to real-life situations/problems/projects? If yes, please explain.*

3. *Does the CSR model curriculum address local community needs in any way? If yes, please explain.*

4. *Does the CSR model curriculum include objectives for developing civic skills and competencies? If yes, please explain.*

5. *Does the CSR model allow students to play a role in planning curricular activities? If yes, please explain.*

6. *Does the CSR model allow teachers to use a variety of learning materials other than textbooks? If yes, please explain.*

7. *Does the CSR model allow teachers to use alternative teaching strategies? If yes, please explain.*

8. *Do the CSR model's instructional methods include project-based learning? If yes, please explain.*

9. *Does the CSR model's curriculum allow teachers to use interdisciplinary team teaching and/or experiential learning methods in teaching? If yes, please explain.*

10. *Are alternative assessments allowed or encouraged? If yes, please explain.*

11. *Does the CSR model address school/district policies regarding students' ability to leave school for outside learning activities? If yes, please explain.*

12. *Does the CSR model allow or provide time for student reflection (journal entries, classroom dialog, discussion)? If yes, please explain.*

Chart on School Model Compatibility with Service-Learning

Survey Question / Models (Rank)*	Rating and Average	Allows teachers to use a variety of learning materials other than textbooks.	Opportunities for students to apply their knowledge/ skills to real-life situations, problems.	Allows alternative assessments, such as portfolios, presentations.	Allows or provides time for student reflection such as journal entries, classroom dialogue.	Instructional methods include project-based learning.
Accelerated (3)	Highly Compatible 4.75	★★★★★	★★★★★	★★★★★	★★★★★	★★★★★
America's Choice (11)	Compatible 3.66	★★★★	★★★★	★★★★	★★★★	★★★★
Atlas Communities (7)	Compatible 4.16	★★★★★	★★★★★	★★★★★	★★★★★	★★★★★
Audrey Cohen College (4)	Highly Compatible 4.58	★★★★★	★★★★★	★★★★	★★★★	★★★★★
Center for Effective Schools (5)	Highly Compatible 4.5	★★★★★	★★★★★	★★★★★	★★★★★	★★★★★
Coalition of Essential (1)	Highly Compatible 5	★★★★★	★★★★★	★★★★★	★★★★★	★★★★★
Community for Learning (7)	Compatible 4.16	★★★★★	★★★★	★★★★★	★★★★	★★★★★
Community Learning Centers (9)	Compatible 3.91	★★★★★	★★★★★	★★★★	★★★★	★★★★★
Co-Nect (5)	Highly Compatible 4.5	★★★★★	★★★★★	★★★★★	★★★★★	★★★★★
Core Knowledge (9)	Compatible 3.91	★★★★★	★★★★★	★★★★★	★★★★★	★★
Different Ways of Knowing (3)	Highly Compatible 4.75	★★★★★	★★★★★	★★★★★	★★★★★	★★★★★
Direct Instruction (12)	Compatible 3.5	★★★★	★★★★★	★★	★★★★	★★★★
Expeditionary/ Outward Bound (2)	Highly Compatible 4.83	★★★★★	★★★★★	★★★★★	★★★★★	★★★★★
Foxfire Fund (14)	Somewhat Compatible 3.08	★★★★	★★★★	★★★★★	★★★★★	★
High Schools That Work (8)	Compatible 4	★★★★★	★★★★★	★★	★★★★	★★★★★
High/Scope (6)	Compatible 4.33	★★★★★	★★★★★	★★★★★	★★★★★	★★★★
Integrated Thematic Instruction (2)	Highly Compatible 4.91	★★★★★	★★★★★	★★★★★	★★★★★	★★★★★

Allows for flexible use of time, e.g. block scheduling.	Allows teachers to use alternative teaching strategies.	Allows teachers to use interdisciplinary team teaching and/or experiential learning methods.	Curriculum addresses local community needs in some way.	Allows students to play a role in planning curricular activities.	Curriculum includes objectives for developing civic skills and competencies.	Addresses school/district policy regarding students' leaving school for outside learning activities.
★★★★	★★★ ★★	★★★ ★★	★★★★	★★★ ★★	★★★★	★★★ ★★
★★★ ★★	★★★★	★★★	★★★★	★★★★	★★★	0
★★★ ★★	★★★ ★★	★★★ ★★	★★★★	★★★★	★★	0
★★★★	★★★★	★★★ ★★	★★★★	★★★ ★★	★★★ ★★	★★★ ★★
★★★ ★★	★★★ ★★	★★★ ★★	★★★ ★★	★★★★	★★★★	★
★★★ ★★	★★★ ★★	★★★ ★★	★★★ ★★	★★★ ★★	★★★ ★★	★★★ ★★
★★★★	★★★ ★★	★★★ ★★	★★★★	★★★★	★★★	★★
★★★★	★★★ ★★	★★★★	★★★★	★★★ ★★	★	★
★★★ ★★	★★★ ★★	★★★ ★★	★★★ ★★	★★★ ★★	★★	★★
★★★ ★★	★★★ ★★	★★★ ★★	★★★★	★★★★	★★	0
★★★ ★★	★★★ ★★	★★★ ★★	★★★ ★★	★★★ ★★	★★★ ★★	★★
★★★★	0	0	★★★ ★★	★★★ ★★	★★★ ★★	0
★★★ ★★	★★★ ★★	★★★ ★★	★★★ ★★	★★★★	★★★★	★★★ ★★
0	★★★★	★★★★	★★★★	★★★ ★★	★	0
★★★★	★★★ ★★	★★★ ★★	★★★★	★★★★	0	★★★ ★★
★★★★	★★★ ★★	★★★ ★★	★★★★	★★★ ★★	★★★ ★★	0
★★★ ★★	★★★ ★★	★★★ ★★	★★★ ★★	★★★ ★★	★★★ ★★	★★★★

Survey Question / Models (Rank)*	Rating and Average	Allows teachers to use a variety of learning materials other than textbooks.	Opportunities for students to apply their knowledge/skills to real-life situations, problems.	Allows alternative assessments, such as portfolios, presentations.	Allows or provides time for student reflection such as journal entries, classroom dialogue.	Instructional methods include project-based learning.
League of Professional Schools (1)	Highly Compatible 5	★★★★★	★★★★★	★★★★★	★★★★★	★★★★★
Learning Network (11)	Compatible 3.66	★★★★★	★★★★	★★★★★	★★★★★	★★★★
MicroSociety (3)	Highly Compatible 4.75	★★★★★	★★★★★	★★★★★	★★★★★	★★★★★
Modern Red Schoolhouse (8)	Compatible 4	★★★★★	★★★★★	★★★★★	★★★★	★★★★★
Onward to Excellence (15)	Neutral 2	★★★★	★★★★	★★★★	★	★★★★
Paideia (4)	Highly Compatible 4.58	★★★★★	★★★★★	★★★★★	★★★★★	★★★★★
QuESt (11)	Compatible 3.66	★★★★	★★★★	★★★★	★★★★	★★★★
Roots and Wings (Success for All) (12)	Somewhat Compatible 3.41	★★★★★	★★★★	★★★★	★★★★★	★★★★
School Development Program (6)	Compatible 4.33	★★★★	★★★★★	★★★★★	★★★★★	★★★★
Talent Development (13)	Somewhat Compatible 3.41	★★★★★	★★★★	★★★	★★★	★★★
Ventures Education Systems Corporation (10)	Compatible 3.75	★★★★	★★★★	★★★★	★★★★	★★★★
Total Averages		4.75	4.67	4.5	4.5	4.36
Total CSRD Rating Per Question		★★★★★	★★★★★	★★★★★	★★★★★	★★★★

SCALE		
4.5 – 5	Highly Compatible	★★★★★
3.5 – 4.4	Compatible	★★★★
2.5 – 3.4	Somewhat Compatible	★★★
1.5 – 2.4	Neutral	★★
0 – 1.4	Not Compatible	★

* Some models have the same score and therefore have the same ranking.

Allows for flexible use of time, e.g. block scheduling.	Allows teachers to use alternative teaching strategies.	Allows teachers to use interdisciplinary team teaching and/or experiential learning methods.	Curriculum addresses local community needs in some way.	Allows students to play a role in planning curricular activities.	Curriculum includes objectives for developing civic skills and competencies.	Addresses school/district policy regarding students' leaving school for outside learning activities.
★★★★★	★★★★★	★★★★★	★★★★★	★★★★★	★★★★★	★★★★★
★★★★	★★★★★	★★★★★	★	★★★★★	★	0
★★★★★	★★★★★	★★★★★	★★★★	★★★★	★★★★★	★★★★
★★★★★	★★★★★	★★★★★	★★★★★	★★	★★	0
★★★★	★	0	★	★	0	0
★★★★★	★★★★★	★★★★★	★★★★★	★★★★★	★★★★★	★★★★★
★★★★	0	★★★★	★★★★	★★★★	★★★★	★★★★
★★★★	★★★★★	0	★★★★	★★★★	★★	0
★★★★	★★★★	★★★★★	★★★★★	★★★★★	★★	★★★★
★★★ ΛΛ	★★★★★	★★★★★	★★	0	★★	★★★★
★★★★	★★★★	N/A	N/A	★	N/A	★★★★
4.36	4.32	4.10	3.96	3.89	3	2.40
★★★★	★★★★	★★★★	★★★★	★★★★	★★★	★

Comprehensive School Reform Demonstration (CSRD) Program Survey

Please help us in this research study. We are looking for areas of compatibility between your CSRD program and general service-learning ideals. One definition of service-learning is community service connected to academics. Service-learning is also described as "bringing real-world meaning and purpose to classroom projects or assignments," and "methodologies that integrate academic and technical skills and applied learning." **Please fax survey back to: Sarah Pearson at 202-775-9733.**

Your answers will be compiled into a study being conducted on the compatibility between CSRD models and service-learning. THIS STUDY IS NOT MEANT TO CRITIQUE THE GENERAL DESIGN OF YOUR CSRD PROGRAM. If you have any questions, please contact Sarah Pearson at American Youth Policy Forum, 202-775-9731, or spearson@aypf.org.
_____ Check here to receive a draft of the report for review via email.

CSRD Program: _____ Program Director: _____ Email: _____

Address/City/State/Zip: _____ Phone/Fax: _____ /

Please name one school that has used your CSRD program for two years: _____ Phone: _____

Questions regarding the use of your CSRD model in school.	5 strong yes	4 yes	3 on the way	2 sort of	1 Don't know/ NA	0 No	Please comment/describe.
1. Does the CSRD model allow for flexible use of time, e.g., block scheduling? If yes, please describe.							
2. Within the CSRD model, are there options for students to apply their knowledge & skills, to real-life situations/problems/projects?							
3. Does the CSRD model address local community needs in any capacity? If yes, please describe.							
4. Does the CSRD model curriculum include objectives for developing civic skills and competencies? If yes, please describe.							
5. Does the CSRD model allow students to play a role in planning curricular activities? If yes, please describe.							

Questions regarding the use of your CSRD model in school.	5 strong yes	4 yes	3 on the way	2 sort of	1 Don't know/ NA	0 No	Please comment/describe.
6. Does the CSRD model allow teachers to use a variety of learning materials other than textbooks? If yes, please describe.							
7. Does the CSRD model allow teachers to use alternative teaching strategies? Please list example(s). If yes, please describe.							
8. Does the CSRD model's instructional methods include project-based learning? If yes, please describe.							
9. Does the CSRD model's curriculum allow teachers to use interdisciplinary team teaching and/or experiential learning methods in teaching? If yes, please describe.							
10. Are alternative assessments allowed or encouraged? e.g., portfolios, presentations or other assessments. If yes, please describe.							
11. Does the CSRD model address school/district policies regarding students' ability to leave school for outside learning activities? If yes, please describe.							
12. Does the CSRD model allow or provide time for student reflection? (journal entries, classroom dialog, discussion on the outcome of projects.)							

Other comments:

Comprehensive School Reform Demonstration (CSRD) Program Survey

Please help us in this research study. We are looking for compatibility between your school's chosen school CSRD program or model and general service-learning ideals. One definition of service-learning is community service connected to academics. Service-learning is also described as "bringing real-world meaning and purpose to classroom projects or assignments," and "methodologies that integrate academic and technical skills and applied learning." **Please fax survey back to: Sarah Pearson at 202-775-9733.**

Your answers will be compiled into a study being conducted on the compatibility between CSRD models and service-learning. THIS STUDY IS NOT MEANT TO CRITIQUE THE GENERAL DESIGN OF THE CSRD PROGRAM. If you have any questions, please contact Sarah Pearson at 202-775-9731, or spearson@aypf.org.

___ Check here to receive a draft of the report for review via email. Faxing any brief statistical information on your school along with the survey would be appreciated.

School Name: _____

Address/City/State/Zip: _____ Principal: _____ Email: _____

Name of CSRD Program/Partner used: _____ Phone/Fax: _____ / _____

Have you used this model for at least two years? ❑ Yes ❑ No

Questions regarding the use of your CSRD model in school.	5 strong yes	4 yes	3 on the way	2 sort of	1 Don't know/ NA	0 No	Please comment/describe.
1. Does the CSRD model allow for flexible use of time, e.g., block scheduling? If yes, please describe.							
2. Within the CSRD model, are there options for students to apply their knowledge & skills, to real-life situations/problems/projects?							
3. Does the CSRD model address local community needs in any capacity? If yes, please describe.							
4. Does the CSRD model curriculum include objectives for developing civic skills and competencies? If yes, please describe.							
5. Does the CSRD model allow students to play a role in planning curricular activities? If yes, please describe.							

Questions regarding the use of your CSRD model in school.	5 strong yes	4 yes	3 on the way	2 sort of	1 Don't know/NA	0 No	Please comment/describe.
6. Does the CSRD model allow teachers to use a variety of learning materials other than textbooks? If yes, please describe.							
7. Does the CSRD model allow teachers to use alternative teaching strategies? Please list example(s). If yes, please describe.							
8. Does the CSRD model's instructional methods include project-based learning? If yes, please describe.							
9. Does the CSRD model's curriculum allow teachers to use interdisciplinary/ team teaching and/or experiential learning methods in teaching? If yes, please describe.							
10. Are alternative assessments allowed or encouraged? e.g., portfolios, presentations or other assessments. If yes, please describe.							
11. Does the CSRD model address school/district policies regarding students' ability to leave school for outside learning activities? If yes, please describe.							
12. Does the CSRD model allow or provide time for student reflection? (journal entries, classroom dialog, discussion on the outcome of projects.)							

Other comments:

A Declaration of Principles

This is an abridged version of the six Principles listed and the action agenda suggested from *The Declaration of Principles: A Review of the Past and Look Toward the Future for Service-Learning and School Reform (National Youth Leadership Council, January 2000)*.

Principle 1: *All Children can achieve higher levels of academic success while learning to serve if they are provided challenging standards and given the opportunity to reach them. Students learn more by serving their communities and their communities prosper as students learn and provide needed service.*

Action: *Continue to set high content and performance standards but, at the same time, provide needed resources and ample opportunities for students to reach the standards.*

Principle 2: *By solving real-life problems, students engaged in service-learning are challenged to exercise leadership and responsibility.*

Action: *Provide realistic and effective opportunities for the voices of youth in decision-making activities at all stages of planning, implementing, and evaluating service-learning initiatives.*

Principle 3: *School improvement and service-learning require career-long teaching and professional development. Successful service-learning programs invariably find innovative ways to advance the twin goals of teacher development and innovative curriculum development.*

Action: *Provide a variety of pre-service and professional development opportunities for all teachers, administrators, and other district and school personnel in order to ensure the knowledge and skills needed to effectively implement service-learning initiatives.*

Principle 4: *Improving our schools requires parental and community involvement. Service-learning provides both teachers and parents with significant roles in helping students bridge the academic skills of the classroom and the responsibilities of daily life.*

Action: *Provide all of those who are involved in service-learning the opportunity to bring their substantial and often unique resources "to the table."*

Principle 5: *Improving our schools requires the participation of the private sector and the full range of every community's resources.*

Action: *Allow all organizations and agencies, public and private, to contribute their knowledge and their human, technical, and—indeed—financial resources. Create strong partnerships, networks, and collaborations that will sustain over "the long haul."*

Principle 6 : *School improvement and service-learning build on the realization that ours is a nation of diverse cultures.*

Action: *Remember that when we state that "we are one people," we are speaking of all students, their parents and families, and their neighbors—regardless of race, ethnicity, gender, age, religion, or disability.*

BIBLIOGRAPHY

American Federation of Teachers. *Seeing progress: A guide to visiting schools using promising programs.* Retrieved 2002, from http://www.aft.org/edissues/rsa/guide/change/seeing.htm.

Anderson, V., & Kinsley, C. (1991). Community service learning and school improvement in Springfield, Massachusetts. *Phi Delta Kappan, 91*(10), 761-765.

Astin, A. W., & Sax, L. J. (1998). How undergraduates are affected by service participation. *Journal of College Student Development, 39*, 251-263.

Austin, S. S., Berceli, C. L., & Mathews, S. (1999). When will I use this stuff anyway? *Mathematics Teacher, 92* (9), 798-799.

Barnett, J., et al. (1997). *Youth consultants. Putting it all together. Linking learning with life.* (ERIC Document Reproduction Service No. ED430133).

Bass, M. (1997). Citizenship and young people's role in public life. *In National Civic Review.* 86, 203-210.

Batchelder, T. H., & Root, S. (1994). Effects of service-learning on undergraduates. *Journal of Adolescene. 17*, 341-355

Belbas, B., Gorak, K., & Shumer, R. (1993). Commonly used definitions of service-learning: A discussion piece. National Clearinghouse of Service Learning.

Bhaerman, R., Cordell, K., & Gomez, B. (1998). *The role of service-learning in educational reform.* Needham, MA: Simon and Shuster, Inc.

Billig, S. H. (2000). Research on K-12 school-based service-learning. *Phi Delta Kappan, 81*(9), 658-665.

Boal, J. T. (2001, Winter). Service-learning. *Creative Living,* 3-7.

Boyte, H., & Hollander, E. (1999). *Wingspread declaration on renewing the civic mission of the American research university.* Providence, RI: Campus Compact.

Boyte, H. C., & Farr, J. (1997). *The work of citizenship and the problem of service-learning, Experiencing citizenship: Concepts of models for service learning in political science.* Washington, DC: AAHE.

Brandes, B., & Green R. (2000). *Off their rockers into service. Connecting the generations through service-learning. Linking learning with life.* (ERIC Document Reproduction Service No. ED430134).

Brandt. R. (1998). *Powerful learning.* Alexandria, VA: Association of Supervision and Curriculum Development. Retrieved 2002, from http://www.ascd.org/readingroom/books/brandt98book.html.

Brill, C. L. (1994). The effects of participation in service-learning on adolescents with disabilities. *Journal of Adolescence, 17*, 369–380.

Bringle, R. G., & Hatcher, J. A. (1995). A service-learning curriculum for faculty. *Michigan Journal of Community Service Learning,* 2, 112-122.

Bringle, R. G., & Hatcher, J. A. (1999). Reflection in service learning: Making meaning of experience. *Educational Horizons, 77* (4), 179-185.

Buchanan, R. L. (1998). Integrating service-learning into the mainstream: A case study. *Michigan Journal of Community Service Learning,* 5, 114-119.

Chambers, L. W., Hoey, J., & Underwood, J. (1998). Integration of service, education, and research in local official public health agencies. *American Journal of Public Health, 88*, 1102 –1104

Chapin, J. R. (1998). Is service-learning a good idea? Data from the national longitudinal study of 1998. *Social Studies, 89*(5), 205-211.

Chapin, J. R. (1999). Missing pieces in the service learning puzzle. *Educational Horizons, 77* (4), 202-207.

Checkoway, B. (2000). Combining service and learning on campus and in the community. *Phi Delta Kappan, 77* (9), 600-606.

Clark, P. G. (1999) Service-learning education in community-academic partnerships: Implication for interdisciplinary geriatric training in the health professions. *Educational Gerontology, 25* (7), 641-660.

Cleary, C. (1998). Steps to incorporate service-learning into an undergraduate course. *Journal of Experiential Education, 2(*3), 130-133.

Cohen, S., & Sovet, C. A. (1989). Human service education, experiential learning and student development. *College Student Journal, 23*, 117–122.

Cooper, D. (1998). Reading, writing and reflection. R. Rhoads, & J. Howard (Ed). *Academic service-learning: A pedagogy of action, and reflection*, pp. 47-56, San Francisco: Jossey-Bass.

Cousins, E., & Mednick, A. (Eds.) (1999). *Service at the heart of learning. Teachers' writings.* Dubuque, Iowa: Kendall/Hunt Publishing Company.

Crawford, M. (2001). *Teaching contextually: Research, rationale, and techniques for improving student motivation and achievement in mathematics and science.* Waco, TX: CCI Publishing.

Des Marias, J., Yang, Y, & Farzanehkia, F. (2000). Service-learning leadership development for youths. *Phi Delta Kappan, 81*(9), 678–681.

Dewey, J. (1897). ARTICLE I: What education is, my pedagogic creed. *The School Journal, LIV*(#), 77-80.

Donahue, D. M. (1999) Service-learning for pre-service teachers: Ethical dilemmas for practice. *Teaching & Teacher Education, 15*(6), 685–695.

Driscoll, A., Holland, B., Gelmon, S., & Kerrigan, S. (1996). An assessment model for service-learning: Comprehensive case studies of impact on faculty, student, community and institution. *Michigan Journal of Community Service and Learning, 5*, 66–71.

Dubois, D. L., & Neville, H. A. (1997). Youth mentoring: Investigation of relationship characteristics and perceived benefits. *Journal of Community Psychology, 25*, 227–234.

Duke, J. I. (1999). Service Learning: Taking mathematics into the real world. *Mathematics Teacher, 92* (9) 794–796.

Dunlap, M. R. (1998). Methods of supporting students' critical reflection in courses incorporating service-learning. *Teaching of Psychology, 25*, 208–09

Dunlap, M. R. (1998). Adjustment and developmental outcomes of students engaged in service-learning. *Journal of Experiential Education, 21*(3), 147–153.

Education Commission of the States (2000). *Service-learning and standards: Achieving academic excellence by serving communities.* Denver, CO: Education Commission of the States.

Fisher, B. J., & Finkelstein, M. S. (1999) The gerontology practicum as service-learning. *Educational Gerontology*, *25*(5), 393–409.

Flannery, D., & Ward, K. (1999). Service learning: A vehicle for developing cultural competence in health education. *Journal of Health and Behavior*, 23, 323–331.

Furco, A. & Billig, S.H. (Eds.) (2002). *Service-learning the essence of the pedagogy. A volume in advances in service-learning research.* Greenwich, CT: Information Age Publishing.

Gough, P. B. (2000). Getting real. *Phi Delta Kappan*, *81*(9), 642–644.

Grantmaker Forum on Community and National Service (2000, April). *Profiles of success: Engaging young people's hearts and minds through service-learning.* Retrieved 2002, from http://www.gfcns.org/gfcns/publications/index.html.

Greene, D. (1998). Reciprocity in two conditions of service learning. *Educational Gerontology*, *24*, 411–424.

Hallen, M. (1991). Gadugi: A model of service-learning for Native American communities. *Phi Delta Kappan, 72*(10) 754–759.

Hargrove, G. P. (1993). Neighborhood Center Perspectives on Community Service Learning. *Equity & Excellence in Education*, *26*, 35–40.

Harkavy, I., & Romer, D. (1999). Service learning as an integrated strategy. *Liberal Education, 85*(3), 14–19.

Herman, R. (Project Director) (1999). *An educator's guide to schoolwide reform.* Retrieved 2002, from http://www.aasa.org/issues_and_insights/district_organization/Reform/index.htm.

Holland, B. (1997). Analyzing institutional commitment to service: A model of key organizational factors. *Michigan Journal of Community Service Learning*, *4*, 30–41.

Hollander, E. L. (1999). *Picturing the engaged campus service and learning: Involving students in civic engagement and responsibility.* Providence, RI: Campus compact.

Hornbeck, D. (2000). Service-learning and reform in the Philadelphia public schools. *Phi Delta Kappan, 81*(9), 665.

Kahne, J., & Westheimer, J. (1996). In the service of what? *Phi Delta Kappan*, *77*(9), 592–600.

Keith, N. Z. (1994). School-based community service: Answers and some questions. *Journal of Adolescence*, *17*, 311–320.

Kesler, L. & Eyring, E. M. (1999). Service-learning general chemistry: Lead paint analysis. *Journal of Chemical Education, 76*(7), 920–923.

Kielsmeier, J. C. (2000). A time to serve, a time to learn. *Phi Delta Kappan*, *81*(9), 652–658.

Krystal, S. (1998). The nurturing potential of service learning. *Educational Leadership, 56*(4), 58–61.

Lansam, G. D. (1999). Development of a service-learning program. *American Journal of Pharmaceutical Education, 63* (1), 41–45.

Lena, H. F. (1995). How can sociology contribute to integrating service learning into academic curricula? *American Sociologist, 26*, 107–117.

Likona, T., Schaps, E., & Lewis, C. (1997). *Eleven principles of effective character education.* Washington, DC: Character Education Partnership.

McCarthy, A. M., & Tucker, M. L. (1999). Student attitudes toward service-learning: Implications for implementation. *Journal of Management Education, 23*(5), 554–73.

McGowan, T. G., & Blankenship, S. (1994). Intergenerational experience and ontological change. *Educational Gerontology, 20,* 589–604.

McMahon, R. (2000) *Service learning: Perceptions of preservice teachers.* (ERIC Document Reproduction Service No. ED431678).

Melchior, A. (1999) *Summary report: national evaluation of Learn and Serve America.* Waltham, MA: Center for Human Resources, Brandeis University.

National Association of Partners in Education, Inc. (1996). *Service-learning and school-to-work: A partnership strategy for education renewal. Results from the Wingspread Summit.* Alexandria, VA: NAPE.

National Commission on Service-Learning (2002). *Learning in deed–the power of service-learning for American schools.* Education Development Center, Newton, MA. Retrieved 2002, from http://www.learningindeed.org.

National Youth LeadershipCouncil (2000, January). *The declaration of principles: A review of the past adn look toward the future for service-learning and school reform. A joint declaration of the Corporation for National Service and the United States Department of Education.* St. Paul, MN: NYLC.

No Child Left Behind, Public Law 107-110 (2002, January 8). Retrieved 2002, from http://www.ed.gov/legislation/ESEA01/.

Palmer, P. J. (1987). Community, conflict and ways of knowing: Ways to deepen educational agenda. *Change,* 5, 20–25.

Parker-Gwin, R. (1996). Connecting service to learning: How students and communities matter. *Teaching Sociology,* 24, 97–101.

Paulins, V. A. (1999). Service learning and civic responsibility: The consumer in American society. *Journal of Family and Consumer Sciences: From Research to Practice, 91* (2), 66–72.

Pickeral, T., & Myers, L. (2001). Service-learning and character education: One plus one is more than two. An issue paper. Denver, CO: Education Commission of the States. Retrieved 2002, from http://www.ecs.org/clearinghouse/24/81/2481.htm.

Putnam, R. D. (1995). Bowling alone: America's declining social capital. *Journal of Democracy, 6*(1), 65–78.

Raskoff, S. (1997). Group dynamics in service-learning: Guiding student relations. *Michigan Journal of Community Service Learning, 4,* 109–115.

Reeb, R. N., Katsuyama, R. M., Sammon, J. A., & Yoder, D. S. (1998). The community service self-efficacy scale: Evidence of reliability, construct validity, and pragmatic utility. *Michigan Journal of Community Service Learning,* 5, 48–57.

Rice, K. L., & Brown, J. R. (1998). Transforming educational curriculum and service-learning. *Journal of Experiential Education, 21* (3), 140–146.

Richardson, S. (1999). *Service-learning teacher training manual. A guide for trainers to help teachers use service learning within the curriculum.* (ERIC Document Reproduction Service No. ED434856).

Riley, R. W., & Wofford, H. (2000). The reaffirmation of 'the declaration of principles.' *Phi Delta Kappan, 81*(9), 670–673.

Rocker, D. (1994). School-based community service: a British Perspective. *Journal of Adolescence, 17*, 321–326.

Roper Starch Worldwide, Inc. (November, 2000). *Public attitudes toward education and service-learning.* New York, NY: Academy for Educational Development.

Rosenberg, S. L., McKeon, L. M., & Dinero, T. E. (1999). Positive peer solutions: One answer for the rejected student. *Phi Delta Kappan, 81*(1) 114–118.

Ryan, D., & Kirkland, D. (1998). Using service-learning in the public speaking class. *Inquiry, 2*(1), 42–46.

Saunders, M. D. (1998). The service learner as researcher: A case study. *Journal on Excellence in College Teaching, 9*(2), 55–67.

Scans 2000 The Workforce Skills Website. Retrieved 2002, from http://www.scans.jhu.edu/NSN/HTML/Skills.htm.

Shumer, R. (1994). Community-based learning: Humanizing education. *Journal of Adolescence, 17*, 357–367.

Shumer, R. (2000). *Service, social studies, and citizenship: Connections for the new century.* (ERIC Document Reproduction Service No. ED430907).

Silcox, H. C., & Leek, T. E. (1997). International service-learning. *Phi Delta Kappan, 78*(8), 615–619.

Skinner, R., & Chapman, C. (1999, September). Service-learning and community service in K-12 public schools. *Statistics in brief.* Washington, DC: National Center for Education Statistics, U.S. Department of Education.

Small, R. V., & Venkatesh, M., & Marsden, J. (1998). *The education of IT professionals: Integrating experiential learning and community service.* (ERIC Document Reproduction Service No. ED431428).

Smink, J., & Duckinfield, M. (2000). *Making the case for service-learning. Action research & evaluation guidebook for teachers.* (ERIC Document Reproduction Service No. ED430141).

Student Service Alliance (2000). *Maryland's best practices: An improvement guide for school-based service-learning.* (ERIC Document Reproduction Service No. ED435554).

Stukas, A. A., Snyder, M., & Clary, E. G. (1999). The effects of "mandatory volunteerism" in intentions to volunteer. *Educational Horizons, 77*(4), 194–201.

Taub, D. J. (1998). Building community on campus: Student affairs professionals as group workers, *Journal for Specialists in Group Work, 23*, 411–423.

Tenenbaum, I. M. (2000). Building a framework for service-learning. *Phi Delta Kappan, 81*(9), 666–670.

Tucker, B., et al. (1999). *What is reflection? Process evaluation in three disciplines.* (ERIC Document Reproduction Service No. ED404933).

U.S. Department of Education. *Compact for Learning.* Retrieved 2002, from http://www.ed.gov/pubs/Compact/.

U.S. Department of Education. *Implementing schoolwide programs: An idea book on planning.* Retrieved 2002, from http://www.ed.gov/pubs/Idea_Planning/.

U. S. Department of Education, Office of Elementary and Secondary Education (2000). CSR in the field: Final update. Retrieved 2002, from http://www.ed.gov/offices/OESE/compreform/CSR00report.html.

U.S. Department of Education. *Selected profiles of early state implementation efforts*. Retrieved 2002, from http://www.ed.gov/offices/OESE/compreform/profiles.html.

Wade, R. C., Anderson, J. B., Yarbrough, D. B., Pickeral, T., Erickson, J. B., & Kromer, T. (1999). Novice teachers' experiences of community service learning. *Teaching & Teacher Education*, *15*(6), 667–84.

Wade, R. C., & Saxe, D. W. (1996). Community service-learning in the social studies: Historical roots, empirical evidence, critical issues. *Theory and Research in Social Education*, *24*, 331–359.

Wang, M., Haertel, G. D., & Walberg, H.J. (1997). *What do we know: Widely implemented school improvement programs*. A special report issued by the Laboratory for Student Success. Philadelphia, PA: Temple University Center for Research in Human Development.

Warren, K. (1998). Educating students for social justice in service learning. *Journal of Experiential Education*, *21*(3) 134-139.

Warter, E. H., & Grossman, J. M.(2000). An application in developmental-contextualism to service-learning. A. Furco & S. H. Billig (Eds.). *Service-Learning: The essence of the pedagogy.* Greenwich, CT: Information Age Publishing.

Weah, W., Simmons, V. C., & Hall, M. (2000). Service-learning and multicultural/multiethnic perspectives. *Phi Delta Kappan*, *81*(9) 673–676.

Weinberg, A. S. (1999). The university and the hamlets: Revitalizing low-income communities through university outreach and community visioning exercises. *American Behavioral Scientist*, *42*, 800–813.

WestEd Regional Education Laboratory, *Comprehensive school reform: Research based strategies to achieve high standards*, http://www.wested.org/CSR/guidebook.

Williams, S. W. (2000). *Expanding teacher education through service learning handbook.* (ERIC Document Reproduction Service No. ED432547).

Wozniak, J. (1997). *Mathematics and science faculty service learning handbook.* (ERIC Document Reproduction Service No. ED397930).

Yates, M., & Youniss, J. (1998). Community service and political identity development in adolescence. *Journal of Social Issues*, *54*, 495–512.

Youniss, J., & Yates, Miranda (1999). Youth Service and moral–civic identity: A case for everyday morality. *Educational Review*, *11*, 361–376.

Zoerink, D.A., Magafas, A. H., & Pawelko, A. (1997). Empowering youth at risk through community service. *Youth Care Forum*, *26*, 127–138.

Other Sources

Comprehensive School Reform

Comprehensive School Reform Web. http://www.CSRWeb.net/.

Laboratory for Student Success. *State Applications for Comprehensive School Reform Funds.* Online at: http://www.temple.edu/LSS/csr_rfp.htm.

National Clearinghouse on Comprehensive School Reform. http://www.goodschools.gwu.edu/.

National Network of Partnership Schools. http://www.csos.jhu.edu/p2000.

Partnership for Family Involvement. http://pfie.ed.gov.

Southwest Educational Development Laboratory, Database of Schools Awarded CSR Funds. [Online] Available at: http://www.sedl.org/CSR/awards.html.

Service-Learning

Boston TeachNet. www.boston.teachnet.org.
Fifteen service-learning projects outlined in full detail, including curricular and standards connections.

Do Something. www.dosomething.org. A companion site for teachers who want to try the Do Something approach in their classrooms.

Education Commission of the State's Compact for Learning and Citizenship (CLC). www.ecs.org/clc. A collection of Issue Briefs on topics such as citizenship, character education, teacher education, and promising practices.

Learning In Deed. http://www.LearningInDeed.org.

Learn and Serve America, Corporation for National and Community Service. http://www.learnandserve.org/

National Commission on Service-Learning can be reached online at: http://www.servicelearning commission.org/.

National Service-Learning Clearninghouse. http://www.servicelearning.org/. A collection of information and ideas supported by the Corporation for National Service.

National Service-Learning Partnership can be reached online at: http://www.service-learningpartnership.org.

SEANet, the State Education Agency K-12 Service-Learning Network. www.seanetonline.org. Collection of state policy news and other features regarding service-learning.

The Grantmaker Forum on Community and National Service. http://www.gfcns.org.

The Peace Corps' World Wise Schools Initiative's service-learning pages. www.peacecorps.gov/wws/service/index.html. A collection of well-organized curriculum materials.

The School District of Philadelphia's service-learning pages. www.phila.k12.pa.us/teachers/frameworks/projects/index.htm. A collection of project-based learning standards.

What Kids Can Do. www.whatkidscando.org. Dynamic materials mostly from youth, with strong education reform leaders behind the scenes making the curricular and school reform connections.